WITH BEST COMPLIMENTS

BANK ALFALAH

Escape from Oblivion

The Story of a
Pakistani Prisoner of War in India

Ikram Sehgal as Captain, Army Aviation

Escape from Oblivion

The Story of a
Pakistani Prisoner of War in India

IKRAM SEHGAL

OXFORD
UNIVERSITY PRESS

OXFORD
UNIVERSITY PRESS

Oxford University Press is a department of the University of Oxford.
It furthers the University's objective of excellence in research, scholarship,
and education by publishing worldwide in

Oxford New York

Auckland Cape Town Dar es Salaam Hong Kong Karachi
Kuala Lumpur Madrid Melbourne Mexico City Nairobi
New Delhi Shanghai Taipei Toronto

With offices in

Argentina Austria Brazil Chile Czech Republic France Greece
Guatemala Hungary Italy Japan Poland Portugal Singapore
South Korea Switzerland Turkey Ukraine Vietnam

Oxford is a registered trademark of Oxford University Press
in the UK and in certain other countries

Published in Pakistan by Oxford University Press

© Oxford University Press 2012

ISBN 978-0-19-906607-0

Typeset in Minion Pro
Printed in Pakistan by
Printech Quality Printers, Karachi.
Published by
Ameena Saiyid, Oxford University Press
No. 38, Sector 15, Korangi Industrial Area, PO Box 8214,
Karachi-74900, Pakistan.

To
My lovely granddaughters
Amaani and Elena;
Their mother Kashmalaa;
My daughters
Haya and Nefer;
And my son
Zarrar
'You were worth staying alive for!'

CONTENTS

FOREWORD

Escape from Oblivion is a fascinating account of a soldier's experiences of his escape from an Indian Security Prison during the 1971 War in East Pakistan. His days in Calcutta are an interesting account of his endeavours to escape detection and of his eventual success in finding a sanctuary in the United States Consulate. His further travels to New Delhi, Agra, Lucknow, Kanpur, Kathmandu and Rangoon before returning to Dacca, are a fascinating account of his efforts to return to his country.

This book is a realistic account of the tragic effect of the inane policies of Yahya Khan and of his political adviser, Zulfikar Ali Bhutto which led to the 1971 debacle in East Pakistan. That the writer was of mixed parentage—a West Pakistani father and an East Pakistani mother—makes it all the more interesting. Ikram Sehgal's sentiment in such a situation deserve sympathy and understanding. His efforts to escape from Indian custody at great risk to his life is a tribute to his loyalty to his country and to the courage of his convictions.

Escape from Oblivion would make an excellent film which could also include the role of a military dictator and his political advisers who led Pakistan to a civil war and to its inevitable consequences.

Air Marshal (retd.) Asghar Khan

ACKNOWLEDGEMENTS

My gratitude to God for everything.

To my late father, who always gave me tremendous freedom in my expressions and actions, and encouraged me to put them down on paper. It is his inspiration that the reader will perceive between the lines. Someone once said: 'it is good to read between the lines; it tires the eyes less.'

My gratitude to Major Saifullah Khan, one of my interrogators at the HQ ISSC Dacca [Dhaka]. Finding me idle and steeped in self-pity while undergoing the lengthy process of debriefing, he encouraged me to write down my experiences. Having spent a hundred days in enemy custody and then a further eighty-four days of incarceration, one tends to resort to repartee. Saifullah was probably led to inspire me because of the saying: 'an idle mind; a devil's workshop'.

In a perverse way, gratitude is also due to those who were engaged in debriefing me at length, leaving me with plenty of latitude as regards time during the process. If my frustration has crept into the soul of this book and if it becomes torturous to read on, you know where to put the blame.

Gratitude to all who helped me, knowingly and unknowingly, in my long journey back home—whoever and wherever they may be. Friends in times of need are friends indeed! To all the clerks who took the trouble in typing out the first draft manuscript. I still have the original draft that was typed on rice paper with a manual typewriter. Anyone who has seen my handwriting will understand what pains they must have taken to bring sense out of chaos. Someone once remarked that my handwriting is reminiscent of a drunken ant dipped in ink and has walked all over the page.

All events and observations narrated in the book are personal. I bear malice towards none—except towards the Indians—and them too for that time only. Before I became a POW in India I regret that I generally believed in General Custer's remark: 'the only good Indian is a dead Indian'. Looking back, it was very immature of me. The fact remains that there are a lot many good Indians out there and I am proud that they consider me a friend. Among them, particular mention must be made of Rati and DhruvSawhney, Princess Jeet and NandKhemka, Pheroza and Jamshed Godrej, Bunty and Pawan Singh Ahluwalia, among a host of others. What really touched me was when the Confederation of India Industry elected in 2005 invited me to be on their World Economic Forum Economic Advisory Board along with four other foreign businessmen from different world regions.

In a way this effort is an eulogy for all the men who fought and died on both sides, Pakistan and Bangladesh, for a dream that became a reality and then turned into a nightmare while I languished for an eternity but comparatively safe in an enemy prison. Such men who fight against all the odds of war are to be eulogized for what they believe in, even if their views and aspirations thereof are contrary to each other. We do not need adjectives to describe them; to posterity, their deeds are eloquent enough. Even if the eventual dream has now become a mirage, the fact remains that it has come back a full circle to the reality of 'two independent sovereign nations', as originally envisaged by the 1940 Lahore Resolution.

Finally, I am aware of the fact that my narrative might not please a lot of people and may even result in controversy, but I have attempted to remain as objective and truthful. At times truth is a bitter pill to swallow but posterity demands that we must come face to face with it. It is my good luck that I am alive to document these events.

Ikram Sehgal

PROLOGUE

Whether he is a common citizen or an ordinary soldier, it is a matter of utmost disgrace for anyone to fall a prisoner into the hands of the enemy. Even when one is mortally wounded, one's last conscious action should be directed towards avoiding this possibility. I make no excuses for myself. I should not have fallen into the trap of my enemy. I hesitated and was lost. I could not do anymore. I was a prisoner. Some people may believe that discretion is the better part of valour. I am afraid I did not feel 'valourous' at the time. My discretion was borne out of cold fear.

In dishonour, I found disgust.

To find myself as a prisoner in enemy country without paying tribute to the name for which I had been trained in a manner which would put any fool to shame. What price, honour?

From the Officer's Mess of Indian 91 BSF (Border Security Force) Battalion I was led handcuffed to their Quarter Guard. It was approximately 8 pm on the night of 7 April 1971, and the place was Agartala. Minutes before, I had been thwarted in my attempt to acquire an automatic weapon from the jeep in which it reposed. Everything had happened in such a swift flourish that I was cursing myself over and over again for being such a fool. Now that I look back, had I been successful in my attempt, my life would have been cut short. A temporary setback must not be regarded as a failure—it can well lead to eventual success. In the cell that I was incarcerated, my legs were also cuffed. I was tied down to the bed with a rope. Someone was not taking any chances. I was covered with blankets and a torch light was being thrown on me. An automatic weapon, an LMG, poked its ugly nose at me through the iron bars of the cell door. It was very melodramatic.

In disgust, I found despair.

Disgust preys on your mind and nerves in such a manner that every nerve-ending cries out in an endless refrain of reproach. When your mind is thus devastated, an eternal frustration reaches out for you.

In despair, I lost fear.

Nothing that matters mattered anymore. When your life is forfeit, you are in servitude. When life itself is of no consequence, the inevitable result is recklessness.

In my struggle to control my fear, I found courage.

Suddenly no shackles can ever hold you down any more. You are swept away by the lonely desolation and you are disconsolate. This is when you have reached the pitch that propels you into your quest for freedom. But what price, freedom?

In the gathering up of my courage, I found my freedom.

Every man likes freedom. He is not a man who is resigned to servitude and confinement. When one is shackled he is forced to observe his surroundings and devise ways and means of breaking them. However, simply craving for freedom is not sufficient. Some other factors are also necessary to compel a man to attempt for freedom. These factors need to be imagined in totality in order to form a picture of the confused and complex workings of the mind and which leads to a lucid, logical execution of a plan whose foundations are primarily a fallout of ones emotions. My original plan failed in many ways; I had to improvise and innovate all the way.

The mental tortures and the physical agonies that I suffered during my days as a prisoner are etched vividly in my mind, but I can never quite express the nightmare of my journey back from the reaches of hell in adequate language. One may feel courageous after the nightmare is over but can one forget the gamut of emotions that one passes through in search of freedom?

A shudder of fear sometimes sweeps through me as I relive, moment to moment, the excitement and the danger of those days. I cannot reproduce those events in mere words—they might sound too theatrical, hence, I will not even attempt to do so. I can simply elucidate some of my hopes, fears and elations that I experienced at the time.

I have gone through an odyssey and yet I am no Ulysses. My belief in God is firm and that is what has sustained me throughout my journey.

I had a date with destiny which I could not avoid.

I have often wondered whether it is justified for us Muslims to call the first day of any military operation 'D Day', or what it signifies in full i.e., 'Doomsday'. I was of the opinion that since we Muslims, if martyred in a battle, are meant to go straight to paradise, is it not appropriate that the first day of the battle be called 'H Day' (Heaven's Day)?

One day before my father's fiftieth birthday and two days before I myself was to reach the stupendous age of twenty-five, I was completely ready to execute the plans made by us to say goodbye to Uppal and his lot. Physically, I was ready to begin the return journey of my Odyssey, although, I cannot draw any comparison with Ulysses as regards my mental faculties. Though my plans had been finalized, I will not hesitate to admit that I was truly petrified.

The meaning of fear is often lost in the wholesome embrace of the word 'courage'. We eulogise courage and deride fear, forgetting in our enthusiasm that courage is actually the control of, and is drawn out of fear. Certain actions which may be borne out of desperation are sometimes labelled as courageous, when in fact, they should be labelled as reckless. There is a deep interplay of courage, fear and recklessness in the emotions of man. There is a certain moment when man, in crossing the rubicon of fear, does not feel either courage or recklessness but the simple determination to achieve what has to be done.

I do not for a moment believe in the occult, yet I am superstitious. Someone had once predicted that it was likely that I might not live to see my twenty-fifth birthday. Although there is no logic to it, but the oriental psyche, regardless of how westernized it may have become, is not able to rid itself of a healthy respect for the supernatural—the result of which was that suddenly my plan of action seemed to be full of flaws. Little trivialities seemed to have been overlooked by me and all my forebodings appeared to be magnified. Every man desires to live; it is useless to proclaim that life is not worth living. People who profess this are hypocrites. Life is always worth living, what needs to be changed are the conditions under which it begins to become unbearable. In order to bring about these changes, risking one's life becomes worth it.

Needless to say I saw death everywhere that day. There would be no second chance to this attempt, and I saw what I presumed to be morbid doubts on the faces of my fellow inmates. When one has reached safety and freedom, one can write brave words but how can one truthfully elucidate the all-encompassing cold fear that sweeps through as the hour of death approaches? Someone has correctly termed it the 'moment of truth'. I love my country and it is no hypocrisy when a man is clear not only about the geographical limits of one's country, but about the ideological leanings that make his country whole. When man possesses such passion, then no sacrifice seems too great. But losing one's life must be worth the sacrifice. Was my sacrifice worth the risk? From the distant reaches of my memory came the command: 'if you have been made a prisoner of war, it is your duty to escape.' One can feel intense fear in being thrown in a position that one was never meant to be . . . in a place where you do not want to die. God and country are true incentives! Pride can be another incentive and to some people a great one. Or was it? Except for Sadiq Nawaz, the others probably thought that I was bluffing!

Anyhow, the die had been cast and the stage was set—all my friends were looking forward to my attempt to escape. By the stroke of circumstance I was now privileged to be the main performer. By nightfall the curtains would be raised. There would be no prompting. Would I measure up to what was expected of me or else swallow my pride and sleep the uncomfortable sleep of a craven coward?

The morning of 16th July was very wet and the weather was atrociously dreadful. I paced up and down my lonely shed: one moment cool, analytical and logical; the next moment confused, feverish and emotionally charged. I repeatedly kept checking, counter-checking my plans and the charted out route of my escape from the camp. I wanted very much to talk to Sadiq, confirm to him that this night was 'IT', but throughout that morning the sentries remained watchful and we avoided interaction.

An Amphibian aircraft which had most likely lost its bearings because of the continuous rain and thick clouds flew low over the camp twice. The sight of that aircraft had a strange affect upon me. Since I am a pilot, this was taken by me as an omen, which was not surprising since I was interpreting everything around me as an omen. 'Two stands for joy'—well, I saw a pair of crows everywhere. A few days earlier, an Alouette-3 helicopter had also flown over the camp in the direction of Calcutta. As the Amphibian flew over above us, Scott who was in the opposite shed ran out to take a look. Since it was raining, he went in to wear his raincoat and came out again. He started talking to the other officers in the adjacent shed across the barbed wire. From time to time he favoured me with contemptuous glances. His aim was very clear: it was to make me sense my loneliness. He succeeded in his aim only too well—he removed any doubt that remained in my mind as to my escape.

The afternoon passed quickly. I ate a light supper and waited for the sheds to be closed. I did finally manage a snatch of conversation with Sadiq, Amjad and Ayaz. I bid a slightly choked farewell to Sadiq who whispered last minute instructions to me. I asked him to inform my parents if anything happened to me during my escape attempt. Shah had also come to know of my plan and came to bid me a sort of a farewell. I admitted to Sadiq that I was petrified. As we embraced each other, I saw tears in his eyes. He said that he would pray for me all night. 'Do not be scared,' he said. 'God will be with you.'

'It is the part of the wise man to forget the inevitable calamities of human life in the enjoyment of the fleeting hour.' Rustam, whose words these are must have known since he was a slave in Persia at a time when the descendants of Sefi made life so unpredictable that a 'man could not depart from the presence of the Sultan without having satisfied himself that his head was still on his shoulders.

For one agonizing moment before the sheds were shut that night, I thought that the game was up. I only realized at that moment the extent of cowardice that a man can experience when he is aware of the fact that his life is hanging by a thread. For just that one single cowardly moment, I actually wanted Scott to discover the missing bolts in the tin sheets which were to provide the opening for my exit from the shed. If Scott had discovered that opening, the matter of the escape would have passed over from my hands. Retribution would have come, but death would have to bide its time. That moment also passed. With venom, Scott kicked at the four corners of the shed to check if anything was loose. He gave orders that one of the corners of the shed should be sealed with bricks the next day. Scott was a most meticulous man and ordered that the fan should be switched off. In his malevolent spite he forgot that the fan and the solitary light in the shed were on the same electricity line. Or was he contemptuously daring me to attempt an escape. I hope for his sake that such was not the case because if it was, then Uppal would never forgive him.

Anyway, giving me a last mirthful smile, he went away. It is human nature to hate a man who is worthy of hate, but to waste one's hate on someone who is utterly inferior is not worth it. He can only feel utter contempt for such a human being. With Scott, so be it! We aspire to teach character-building to the educated by telling them that since they are educated, they have the required tools for inculcating a positive character in themselves. Yet we see that often it is the poor and the uneducated who are possessed with a better character which we ever so often vainly preach. It is the preacher of ideals who most often loses sight of what he is preaching. So who is superior?

I tried to lie down and rest. It was most important for me to be fresh hence I forced myself to relax. But my nerves were taut and it was impossible to loosen up. While there was still some light I stuffed a pillow case with a bush shirt, jacket, vest, *lungi* (loin cloth), slippers and a horseshoe that I had found. Sadiq had told me to take it along for luck.

The soft patter of rain could be heard on the roof. The sound of the falling rain was magnified on the tin roof, but apart from this, all was quiet in the camp. I had noticed that most of the camp personnel had collected in the cookhouse/supply shed. It was Friday night and on this night the weekly quota of rum was issued, or so I had come to understand from Sundarasen's conversation with us. Naik Christopher was the Guard Commander, a quiet and sleepy soul. Naik Pukhraj was the other replacement. Both could be counted upon to take a good swig at the rum and sleep it off. Sundarasen, though friendly, was dangerous because he would invariably check the shed once we were all asleep. Although he was not a rum drinker, he was not on duty on Friday night.

Moments ticked away and the hour came closer. Since there was no watch, the planned time of my escape was to be when I was satisfied that it had become dark enough for me to venture out. I had deliberately chosen to get out early so that by sunrise I would have covered a sizable distance between myself and the camp. This of course depended on the condition that it would rain heavily.

I had to be as silent as possible. I tied up the mosquito net around my bed and set up the bed in such a manner that anyone inquisitive enough to flash a light inside would think that a person was lying there. I tied my *taviz* (amulet) around my wrist. It had been given to me by my grandmother folded in a silken scarf and I always kept it on my person. The Indians had inspected both—they had pried open the *taviz* and had inspected the scarf meticulously. They had probably been worried that it contained a map or some such similar thing as pilots did carry in wartime. They had tried to take it from me but I had been duly emotional about it and they left it alone. This *tavis* was particularly valuable to me at this hour.

I pushed against the loose sheets with my right shoulder. I was wearing only my underwear. The tin sheets made an awful sound. I had already opened up the first loose sheet with the aid of an iron rod, and the second loose sheet with the help of a pillow case so that there was more space for me to get out. But the third sheet was extremely tight and squeezing my way out was very difficult and awkward, and in the process I bruised my shoulders and hip. I had to twist myself around and hence when I managed to get out, I was lying on my back. It was quite a noisy process but thankfully the sentries were far away and the rain on the roof effectively drowned out the noise. But as I tried to bring my whole body out, I made the mistake of also trying to take the iron rod and the pillow case that I had been using as a sort of a jack. As a result, my foot got stuck in a very awkward position. Luckily this was just a momentary annoyance and I managed to get my foot loose. I then rolled sideways onto the wet grass.

Once I was on the grass, I lay completely still for a while in order to orientate myself with my surroundings and take stock of the situation. My immediate concern was to assess whether the sentries had made any untoward movement by the noise that was created while I was struggling to get out of my cell. Although I could not see them, I was able to gauge their position through their voices. The first group of sentries were chatting amiably behind the officer's shed which was screened by the overgrown grass and the newly constructed latrines. The other group of sentries were too far away and not in my line of vision. The main camp opposite was absolutely quiet. A couple of minutes before my exit from the shed, a few vehicles had driven out of the camp. After having satisfied myself and clutching the iron rod and the pillow case, I crawled backwards. I did this to get away from the main road where a regular beat of two sentries would constantly patrol up and down the road in between the inner and outer wire in front of the compound. Although the grass was quite high, it flattened out as I walked on it. I rolled sideways to the right until I had reached the inner wire.

Here I must provide an illustration of my thoughts that were racing in my mind at the time as I remember them. Strangely, I do not remember anything but a vague sense of satisfaction at succeeding in making a comparatively easy exit from the shed. I do not remember feeling scared. I remember no other emotion or sense of elation which could have actually proven to be dangerous. I was thinking coolly and analytically. I could figure out the position of the sentries by their voices but I could still not see them. The two sentries who were at the back of the shed were coming 'in loud and clear' but from the location where I placed the other two sentries to be, which was close to the sentry box with the guard commander which was obscured from view and from this distance, I could only hear murmurs. The remaining pair was too far away for me to bother about. At that time I had no intention of going in that direction. I wedged the iron rod in between the two strands of barbed wire and crawled through. This first crossing through the barbed wire was easy. I was now in the area between the officers and the Junior Commissioned Officer's (JCO) compounds.

I made my way towards the road. I could hear the clicking of boots of the remaining pair of sentries coming towards my direction and I did a backward crawl in record speed. The sentries passed by me on the road but did not favour the area in which I was skulking in even with the cursory glance. When these two had safely gone past, I rolled sideways till I was alongside the wire of the JCO compound. I again made my way towards the road. At this time all the lights in the camp went out.

My original plan had been to cross the road on the outward journey of the two sentries towards the Other Ranks (OR) compounds. In this way I would soon be out of the lit perimeter though I was still within the periphery of the inhabited part of the camp. This would have taken a fairly short time.

As the lights went out, I got up to sprint across the road though there was a fairly large depression filled with water just in front of me. I knew that as soon as the lights went out, the auxiliary generator would start functioning after a gap of about two to three minutes. But I hesitated a moment, some sixth sense made me stop and lie down again. In the meantime the guard commander had flashed his torch a number of times along the road, and the two sentries had turned around in their outward journey and were coming back. The lights came on again within a minute. The instinct that had prevented me from attempting to make a move towards the road had probably saved my life. I have never been more grateful to my instincts as then. I crawled backwards again so that I would be as far away from the road as possible when the sentries passed again.

For some reason, the pair came back and stood opposite me, chatting. I was lying in the overgrown mushy grass along the wire of the JCO compound with the pillow case under my chin, willing them silently to keep moving . . . to go away. They remained there chatting for a minute or two and then looked towards my direction. Was their glance for a moment, or minutes, or hours? To me their gaze seemed to reach into the darkness and transfix in eternity. They were in the light and I could see them clearly, hence, I thought that they could see me too. I still wake up at night, thinking of those two, and wonder why they did not see me? Strange thoughts flitted through my mind as I lay there perfectly still, as I have been taught to do so during stalking. This was my acid test—the acid test for a true soldier. I was merged into my own element, the element of infantry in its apt surroundings. The ground and the darkness were my friends, or my enemies, as I chose to perceive them. My nerves and field craft would decide the issue. For a moment I thought of standing up and surrendering myself before they started shooting because they were looking ever so intently in my direction and I had no doubts about their opening fire on me had they seen me. I knew that if the sentries discovered me outside the shed at night they would shoot—and shoot to kill.

But that moment of weakness also passed and I lay there immersed in cold water, not even daring to shiver.

Picture yourself—lying in the cold, wet grass of Panagarh, with two sentries peering at you, or so you think, from a distance which is less than twenty-five yards from you. It is now drizzling, drops trickling down your face and time is standing still. Thoughts race through your mind . . . extreme despair. You think, 'so this is how it all ends' . . . hoping against hope. Until I breathe, I hope. It is because of hope that you continue to lie there, oblivious of your surroundings, the sound of your breathing harsh, yet not discernable to you. I recite the *Kalima* over and over again. How quickly you entreat God in times of need.

The sentries moved away.

As soon as they went out of my line of sight I squirmed through the wire into the JCO compound. I am afraid that the release from the sustained tension made me nervous and careless, with the result that I cut myself badly by the barbed wire all over my body, especially my feet. My underwear was torn badly. But I could not have cared less. Our training teaches us: '*Do not allow your head to be pinned against the wall.*' It also teaches us: '*Do not remain in one place for too long.*'

This was the first change in my original plan.

I was now in the JCO compound. The grass was quite high and for the moment I was comparatively safe from surveillance. There was a depression along the railway track and I made my way alongside it. I rolled onto the concrete pavement and reached the edge of the shed at the back. I could hear Naib Subedar Aurangzeb and Naib Subedar Painda Khan talking. Through the space in between the twin sheds I made my way towards the road again. But the road here was very well lit up and it would have been quite risky attempting to cross here without attracting attention. I worked my way back to the original place at the back of the shed and took stock of the situation.

Attempting to cross the road or to scale the wall inside the lighted perimeter was out of question. I had to make my way to the flanks. On the side of the officers' compound I could still see the two sentries sitting and chatting merrily. However, I noticed something very interesting. The two sentries who were supposed to be at the back of the OR compound were not there and due to the rain were sitting inside the sentry box on the road. This gave me the flexibility to gravitate towards the OR compound from where I could finally make my way out of the lighted perimeter. While I was thus occupied by my thoughts, the two roving sentries squelched through the mushy grass in between the officers and the JCO compound, passing directly over the place where I had been lying watching them just a few minutes ago. These two have never ceased to mystify me. Did they suspect something at first before giving it up as a silly surprise? Did an afterthought to have another look strike them, hence the later inspection? A soldier who suspects something must never let it pass as a figment of his imagination and must investigate thoroughly howsoever silly one may feel, and even if his suspicions are found to be unjustified. I personally think that these chaps made a belated decision to investigate and made a cursory inspection afterwards. Their hesitation saved my life.

I had now reached the western perimeter wire of the JCO compound. This time I was careful. I removed some bricks which had been used to plug up the depression and moved into the gap between the JCO and OR compound.

Panagarh is full of snakes: the camp was infested with them and all this time I was worried about encountering them. This would not have been poetic justice. Moreover I do not like snakes—I cannot stand the sight of them, let alone coming into intimate contact with them in their own haven.

The choice before me now was whether to go into the OR compound which did not have any grass or risk exposure by going along the wall to the corner of the perimeter and thereby affect an exit. Field Marshal Slim maintains: 'it is better not to have counsel of one's fears,' and subsequently, 'it pays to be bold.' Moreover, 'when in doubt, hit out.' But I will admit that I was paying no heed to any of these words of wisdom at the time.

There was a stack of cut grass lying next to the steel tower and I decided that this would give me adequate cover from the sentries sitting alongside the wall behind the officers' compound about three hundred yards away, still chattering away. God bless them for their incessant conversation. Their voices were like a 'lighthouse' for me: helping me navigate my way through unknown waters. It was not their fault. It is not the first time that vigilance has been compromised by a false sense of complacency developed due to the passing of time. How many times has a battle thus been won by surprise? It depends upon the audacity of man to deliver that surprise. Skorzeny had said that, 'if man be the weapon, the bullet that weapon fires must be surprise.'

The stretch I had to cover along the wall in the lit up perimeter was by far the most difficult that I had to overcome because I was directly under the lights, and if anyone just cared to glance this way, I would have been discovered. The OR latrine and bathroom provided me with some cover as I crawled along the wall in a slight depression. I could now see the two sentries sitting in the wooden sentry box on the road next to the OR compound very clearly. Within a matter of scrambling moments I was behind the searchlight negotiating the outer wire. There was a wooden post with the wall which formed the anchor for the barbed wire. Between the post and the wall, there was enough space to go through. Although I was out of the outer wire, I ran up against an old mesh wire. I negotiated this in the same manner.

I was now beyond the range of the lighted perimeter. This was the extreme corner of the camp which I had not seen before but I knew that this part was uninhabited. I went a bit away from the perimeter and rested just a while before I began to think about my next move. I had moved along the wall before lying down so as to be as far away as possible from the range of the lit up area.

Having rested for a few minutes, I made my way towards the uninhabited area, planning to go through it and out of the railway gate because the wall was quite high. But when I approached it I heard several voices and decided not to press my luck too far and came back to the wall. The wall was about ten feet in height and had no footholds. The question of vaulting it like we did in assault courses did not arise because the height was too much. Although it was not impossible to do so if I had had a running start and the strength to haul myself up. But the overgrowth of grass all around was a hurdle. I therefore searched alongside the wall to see whether there was a drain or a tree which could aid me in jumping over the wall. I finally discovered a tree six inches from the wall, which had branches protruding all over the place and looked promising. For me this tree was just ideal. The wall had spikes jutting outwards on top with three rows of barbed wire strands. I slung my pillow case on the top where it lodged in the wire. I then looked around to check whether all was safe and clear before attempting to climb the tree which I would use as a lever to haul myself over the wall. This was easier said than done. Twice I managed to reach the top but missed my hold and came crashing down; the second time receiving quite a severe jolt. The branches of the tree would bend with my weight and, hence, as soon as I would manage to hold on to the top edge of the wall, I would lose my balance and be back to square one.

I had to think . . . told myself that I must not panic. It is only a tree and the wall is within its range. Remember Robert Bruce and his favourite spider:

If at first you do not succeed, then try and try again. However if at first you do not succeed, then rest, think over the problems and then attempt intelligently.

There I was lying on the grass with the light rain falling on my face, my mind devoid of all thoughts of Indians and snakes. All my thinking energies were spent in how to climb up that tree and get onto the wall. On that evening of July 1971 in Panagarh I was haunted by the ghosts of my military instructors, Capt. Imtiazullah Warriach, Capt. Asghar, my original Platoon Commander in the third term, and our Term Commander Maj. Aziz who had transformed me from a civilian into some semblance of a soldier. I simply had to succeed in getting up that tree.

In my third attempt I managed to climb up the tree as high as I could. When I was high enough to step onto the wall, I did so. I gathered up my pitiful belongings in the pillow case and peered down the wall. In the darkness, all I could see was water and high grass down below. From this height, one could make out that the water was deep. Moreover, I had to go through the barbed wire which was not possible. The only choice was to walk on top of the wall using the barbed wire to steady oneself till I reached the corner. There, while lying down, I undid the knots of the wire and opened them one by one. It took some time but eventually I managed.

I then threw the pillow case down first before jumping down myself. Once I had gathered myself I changed my clothes, putting the *lungi* and vest on while discarding the Pyjama. I then waded about 200 yards through the water till I reached the road.

I again looked at the camp. It was quiet and ominous. I felt I was leaving something behind—and I was.

Goodbye Sadiq! Goodbye my friends!

I am carrying your hopes with me even though you do not know it as yet. I have successfully broken out of an enemy camp. It was something to feel exultant about but there was no time for self-congratulations. I had to move on. I got on to the road; a silent prayer of thanks to God on my lips.

I forgot. There was one chap who would not be very happy at my leaving without farewell. The Commandant of the Indian Prisoner of War Camp, Panagarh, Major R.S. Uppal, OC 430 Field Company, 203 Army Engineer Regiment. He had proclaimed that he would break me and send me out of the camp on my knees. He was right, I did go out on my knees but on my own terms and at the time of my own choosing.

I looked again at the camp.

Goodbye Uppal, dear chap, it was not nice knowing you!

1

91 BORDER SECURITY FORCE

The Indian subcontinent was the 'Jewel in the Crown' of the British Empire until the time of independence in August 1947, when the British had to yield to the demands of the native population and leave India. The Muslims, led by our charismatic leader Mohammad Ali Jinnah opted for a separate homeland from the Hindu populace and, hence, the creation of two nations: Pakistan and India. The finest experiment of nationhood in its time, Pakistan comprised of two Wings—East and West Pakistan—separated by nearly 1500 miles of hostile Indian territory. West Pakistan comprised of Sindh, Balochistan, Punjab and North-West Frontier Province [now Khyber Pakhtunkhwa]. In the greatest migration known to mankind, nearly 15 million people were displaced, with large numbers of Muslims leaving India for the two Wings of Pakistan and reciprocally, Hindus and Sikhs leaving Pakistan for India. But the Partition resulted in tragic killings of multitudes on both sides of the border. Nearly 1.5 million were massacred. These killings added to the already prevailing Hindu-Muslim animosities. Hence, tensions between India and Pakistan began almost from the infancy of the newly born countries. With India initially blocking payments to Pakistan from the joint Sterling account, Pakistan was bitter over the distribution of financial assets left by the British. There was also concern arising from question of the accession of the Princely States to India or Pakistan. Although almost all of these states made their choices swiftly but some, due to their geographic location and the religious majority of their populace, delayed the decision over the choice of the country. One such state was Hyderabad [Deccan]. Hyderabad is a landlocked state in the south of India which had a pre-dominantly Hindu majority population but with a Muslim ruler (Nizam) who was not willing to accede to India. But India resorted to force and the Nizam finally had to succumb and hence Hyderabad became part of Indian territory. Having a Muslim majority but a Hindu Raja (king), Kashmir shared borders with both India and Pakistan. The first war between

India and Pakistan was fought over Kashmir in 1947–48 when Kashmir's Raja decided to accede to India. The United Nations intervened and Kashmir was divided by a Cease Fire Line (CFL) demarcating Kashmir into Pak-Administered Kashmir, and Jammu & Kashmir which was given to India. Although the UN Security Council decided in a UN Resolution in 1949 that a plebiscite be held and the Kashmiri people should be given the right to decide their fate, to date, India refuses to abide by the resolution. Yet another war was fought over the dispute in 1965 between the two countries.

Almost from the time of Pakistan's inception, East Pakistan felt systematically deprived of its share in the country's governance and the military. Both establishments were dominated by the West Wing. The language movement of 1952 also played its part in creating tensions between the two Wings, as majority Bengalis very rightly demanded Bengali as their official language in place of Urdu. The next decade saw the continued increase in dissatisfaction with the Central Government over economic and cultural issues and the Awami League (AL) emerged as the political voice of the Bengalis. In the 1960s, when the AL, under the leadership of Sheikh Mujibur Rahman began to demand autonomy, Mujib was jailed in 1966 for charges of hatching a conspiracy. This came to be known as the famous 'Agartala Conspiracy Case'. He was released in 1969 after a popular uprising in East Pakistan. The Central Government gave further cause for dissatisfaction to the Bengali populace by responding in an insensitive manner to the devastating cyclone that hit East Pakistan in 1970.

The year 1970 witnessed the first really free and fair elections in Pakistan's history. The Awami League enjoyed a monopoly of popularity in East Pakistan. In the elections, under Mujibur Rahman, the party won a majority in the 313 seats in the Parliament and claimed the right to form a government. The Pakistan Peoples Party under the leadership of Zulfikar Ali Bhutto won majority votes in West Pakistan. Bhutto refused to accept the premiership of Mujibur Rahman. This refusal by vested interests in West Pakistan to allow the Awami League to form a government, as was their due right, contributed in further alienating the East and West Pakistanis.

Between 2 March 1971 and 25 March 1971, a standoff prevailed, with the entire population of East Pakistan in a state of open defiance; the Army holed up in their cantonments behind barricades. Many excesses were perpetrated in the East Wing on West Pakistanis and on the non-Bengali population during this period in isolated areas. This caused a lot of anger among the non-Bengali element in the Pakistan Army, both in East and West Pakistan. This also convinced the [then] President General Yahya Khan that it was imperative to suppress the East Pakistani insurgency. Due to shortage of military units of purely West Pakistani origin, units of non-Bengali origin were flown in from West Pakistan to augment the division, in addition to the Pakistan Army's Eastern Command contingent that was present in East Pakistan. It was attempted that the Bengali units are kept at bay. This lack of trust as regards their loyalty eroded whatever fealty they felt towards a united Pakistan. Although there were still many who were not convinced that both Wings needed to completely break away from each other. By the end of February 1971, more than a brigade plus had been flown in to reinforce the depleted Infantry Division in East Pakistan.

After several days of shut-down strikes and non-cooperation movements, on the night of 25 March 1971, the Pakistani military cracked down on Dacca [Dhaka], the capital of East Pakistan. There were large scale arrests of dissidents and attempts were made to disarm soldiers and police personnel of East Pakistani origin. The Awami League was banished; many of its leaders went into exile to India. Sheikh Mujibur Rahman was arrested on 25 March 1971[1] and flown to West Pakistan.

The Pakistan Army launched a violent operation in East Pakistan to restore law and order which resulted in many deaths, both military and civilian. They also attempted to disarm the units of the East Bengal Regiment. The East Pakistan Rifles (EPR), a para-military force, led the rebellion in many areas. In Chittagong, Major Rafique launched the revolt on 26 March. He was at least a day ahead of *Major Ziaur Rahman who revolted on 27 March 1971 and declared East Pakistan's independence and the creation of the new state of Bangladesh on the radio from a radio station at Kalurghat.

The core of the rebellion were the regular units of the Pakistan Army, comprising almost 100 per cent Bengali personnel, namely, 2E Bengal (Joydebpur), 4E Bengal (Comilla), and 8E Bengal (Chittagong). All three succeeded in withdrawing to the Eastern borders and concentrated in Sylhet, Comilla and the Chittagong Hill Tracts and surrounding areas. While they acted superbly so did the units of the Pakistan Army which was given the dual task of subduing the dissent and pursuing the dissidents. On the western side of the East Pakistan border, the rebels

---

*Major Ziaur Rahman belonged to the 8th Battalion of the East Bengal Regiment (8E Bengal) of the Pakistan Army.

were joined by 3E Bengal (Rangpur) and the Rifle Companies of 1E Bengal (Jessore) that survived the attempt to disarm them. Bengali officers and men from other fighting arms and services of the Pakistan Army joined them, as well as Bengali officers and men from the Pakistan Air Force (PAF) and Navy. They, along with the officers of EPR, formed the core of the Mukti Bahini. My own parent battalion, 2E Bengal, which my father had raised as a Major on 7 February 1949, was located in Joydebpur which was 26 miles north of Dacca. While the Battalion HQ and two companies remained in Joydebpur, one Rifle Company each had been sent to Tangail and Mymensingh for Internal Security (IS) duties. Faced with being disarmed on the morning of 28 March 1971, the unit revolted on the night earlier, i.e., on 27 March. This resulted in the unnecessary killings of Pakistani officers that were serving with them which is a blot on their otherwise outstanding reputation as an infantry unit.

After a brief advance by two rifle companies (augmented by an EPR company) towards Dacca through Narsingdi, the unit under the command of Major Shafiullah went by road to Mymensingh and then by rail to Bhairab Bazaar. From there they moved by road to the Telipara Tea Estate on the Sylhet-India border. They were joined there by 4E Bengal from Brahmanbaria. The Indians poured in men and material help through their Border Security Force (BSF). They actively joined in to aid in the revolt. The Indians opened the borders allowing approximately 10 million people to flee East Pakistan and seek shelter in refugee camps established by the governments of West Bengal, Bihar, Assam, Meghalaya and Tripura.

Agartala, situated in a plain along the Haora River, is the capital of the Indian state of Tripura. It is located at 2 kilometers from the railway junction town of Akhaura in the Comilla district of Bangladesh. In 1970 the capital of the then Princely State of Swadhin Tripura was at Rangamati (Udaipur, South Tripura).The capital was shifted by Maharaja Krishna Kishore Manikya to Agartala to a place called Old Haveli. The eventual process of shifting the capital from Old Haveli to New Haveli (present Agartala) had started in 1849. During the British period, Agartala was the capital of the erstwhile 'Hill Tippera' State; Agartala Municipality being established during the reign of Maharaja Bir Chandra Manikya (1862–1896) within an area of 3 sq. miles. In 1971, its population was approximately 100,000. Since the population of the city is mainly Bengali, their language predominates, though there is also a growing population of the native Tripuri people in the city.

Agartala Airport (now Singerbhil Airport) is located 12 km (6.5 nautical miles) southeast of the city. During World War II, the airport was used as a supply point by the United States Army Force, 10th Air Force, 4th Combat Cargo Group, which flew C-46 Commando transport aircrafts over Burma. The unit air-dropped pallets of supplies and ammunition to the advancing Allied Forces on the ground in Burma. Agartala was also significant to the history of the region as it was here that close aids of Sheikh Mujibur Rahman, populist leader of East Pakistan reportedly held clandestine meetings with Indian leaders and Indian intelligence agents from RAW, leading to the infamous Agartala Conspiracy Case. This eventually led to the separation of East Pakistan from its Western Wing and the emergence of Bangladesh as an independent nation, with Sheikh Mujubur Rahman as its founding father.

I had reached Dacca on 27 March 1971 on posting to Logistic Flight, Eastern Command and was on 'joining time' and as such free to do as I pleased. I was informed that orders were waiting for me to go back to West Pakistan and join the Army Aviation contingent that was being sent to Sri Lanka to assist the Sri Lankan Armed Forces against the Janatha Vimukthi Peramuna (JVP) terrorist movement. In the meantime, I was told to continue with my 'joining time' till I formally received my orders. At that time Dacca was a killing zone, and with a Punjabi father and Bengali mother, it was an emotional minefield for me.

In choosing to go to 2E Bengal in Joydebpur I had been led by my heart and not with my mind. It was to find out for myself after they had revolted on 28 March 1971, whether all that was being alleged against the 2E Bengal was true. I went to my immediate Flight Commander Major Patrick Tierney and informed him that since I was on 'joining time' for ten days, I would like to go meet my unit, the 2E Bengal. Although Patrick Tierney thought it was a terrible idea on my part under the circumstances and that I would most likely be killed, upon my insistence, he reluctantly gave me permission. I was sanctioned some weapons by Major Liaquat Bokhari and for my protection, my batman Mostafa (from 7E Bengal), who had come with me from Karachi to Dacca, accompanied me. Mostafa was from Chittagong and could speak Bengali fluently but he was of Bihari descent. I borrowed the car of the ADC to the Commander Eastern Command and attempted to get to Joydebpur by road. However, due to road blocks, I had to make my way on foot and by getting onto a rail trolley to Brahmanbaria where 4E Bengal was posted. By this time even they had revolted. After a brief stopover with them, I eventually reached 2E Bengal at Bhairab Bazaar. This regiment had revolted on the night of 27 March at Joydebpur and moved by road to Mymensingh where one Rifle Company was already located on Internal Security duties. On the way they took along a Rifle Company located in Tangail. From Mymensingh they took a train to Kishoreganj. By the time I reached my unit, my world had been turned topsy-turvy—the writing clearly on the wall. One could never believe that the 2E Bengal had killed their West Pakistani colleagues. Sadly, it was true. The massacre of the family of Subedar Ayub was especially heinous and unforgivable. All these officers had repeatedly been warned by West Pakistani officers that they would be killed if they did not leave the unit. During those critical days, some Bengali officers even advised them to take leave or go to Dacca on some pretext. All of them—without exception—refused to take the easy exit by abandoning the unit. It was unthinkable on their part to do so, particularly at such a juncture. They all were of the sentiment that if they stood their ground, they will be able to stop any action that might be taken against their unit. But they proved to be gravely wrong. They were murdered—their martyrdom proves that they were heroes by all means. Their killing is a dark stain on history and can never obliterate the fact that they were a fine battalion.

In Bhairab Bazaar, I realized that my romantic notion: 'Glory and honour of the regiment must come first', had been shattered. In spite of this, how can one ever forget the vociferous adulation that the entire unit bestowed on me on 31 March 1971.

Their 'Chand Sahib' was back!

Till today I have not been able to get over the incongruity of it. A Punjabi officer being cheered by Bengali soldiers surging with emotion in the middle of a civil war based on racial hatred between Punjabis [all West Pakistanis were called Punjabis] and Bengalis. The look of envy on the faces of the some of the younger Bengali officers in the unit said it all.

I was a dead man.

The question was when?

Three West Pakistani officers had already been killed since that was the only way to ensure that a revolt is aroused and I was clearly expendable in the eyes of the younger lot. For me the choice no longer remained in my hands. It was destiny that had brought me here to the unit I loved, even though I loved Pakistan from the very core of my

Ikram Sehgal standing next to an Alouette 3 in Azad Kashmir

PANAGARH POW CAMP

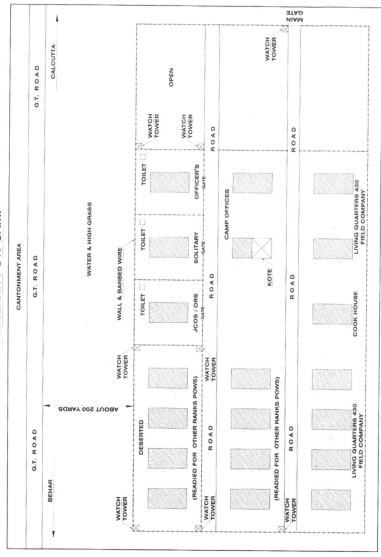

Ikram Sehgal with Sehgal Company, 4 Sindh (formally 44 Punjab), Malir Cantonment, Karachi (2007)

Ikram Sehgal and daughter Nefer with 2E Bengal in Dhaka (2008)

being. I was now left with no choice but to die in uniform among my troops whom I loved.

When Lt. Col. M.H. Khan was removed from command on 21 March 1971, Lt. Col. Raquib [a Bengali officer] had been brought from 32 Punjab by Brig. Jahanzeb Arbab, Comd. 57 Brigade, to take over the unit. When the unit revolted they left Col. Raquib behind and Maj. K.M. Shafiullah took over as the Officiating CO. Maj. Shafiullah, who had served as my father's adjutant, immediately gave me my last command in 2E Bengal, Bravo Company, the original company commanded both by my father and myself. He put Alpha Company with Nasim and a Company also temporarily under my command. During the Civil War that broke out in East Pakistan later on, Major Shafiullah was one of its Sector Commanders. And after the creation of the independent country of Bangladesh, he became its Army Chief and remained so till Sheikh Mujibur Rahman was assassinated on 15 August 1975. A military coup took place and Major Shafiullah was retired; his post as COAS taken over by Maj. Gen. Ziaur Rahman.

On 5 April 1971, when I refused to cross over into India, officers became doubtful whether my men would agree to cross over without me. However, except for a handful of 2E Bengal officers, there was no doubt among the rebel officers that they could not take the risk of testing my loyalty. Elements of a revolt within a revolt was being sensed. There was obviously a difference of opinion about what should be done to me—those who really cared for me—officers like Shafiullah, Shishu and Nasim did not want that I should be killed. Although I was not privy to all this, the tension among the younger officers was quite palpable, but they were powerless to take any action in the presence of the rank and file of 2E Bengal. Obviously there would be trouble in the unit if they touched me there hence I was cleverly lured away from my Company by being told that Col. MAG Osmany,[2] who was soon to become General and Commander-in-Chief of Mukti Bahini, wanted to meet me near the border. I was lulled by the fact that a squad from No. 6 Platoon B Company, 2E Bengal, was to accompany me and I was taken under the escort of Major Khaled Mosharraf.

Major Khaled Mosharraf who was by now CO 4E Bengal, had been suspicious of me right from the time I reached him in Brahmanbaria. He had asked Maj. Shafiullah on wireless whether he should 'dispose' of me but Shafiullah had told him bluntly that he would have to answer to 2E Bengal if even a hair on my body was touched. Khaled Mosharraf kept quietly casting doubts about me which aroused the younger officers against me when the two units gathered in Teliapara Tea Estate. He had suggested to Col. Osmany that I should be inducted into his staff. While Shafiullah was reluctant, Khaled Mosharraf convinced him that it was in my interest to at least meet Col. Osmany. When we reached the border Mosharraf said that we had to go on to the camp where Col. Osmany was. The camp was near Agartala. The jeeps carrying my escort of 2E Bengal troops were stopped somewhere, I did not realize it till we had reached 91 BSF. There I was to be handed over to 91 BSF. The 2E Bengal was to be told that I was seriously wounded during the journey to Agartala and was being taken care of in a hospital.

Destiny had made my choice for me, I was a Pakistani and a Prisoner of War (POW) in Indian custody. There is no rationale for this. However one thing was certain, for me the debt of love for 2E Bengal was complete, from now on our ways were separate, that is, if I could make it out alive. I admit that I lay awake that night in acute discomfort and cold fear. But I was so drained of emotions that I did have a fitful sleep. In the morning I found that I was sharing my dwellings with two others. Later I came to know their names, Anil and Tapan, and the circumstances of their confinement in a cell. They were two self-confessed AWOLs (Absent Without Leave) who had been awaiting punishment for the last 40 days. However, both of them were quite cheerful, and I at least had some human company for the first two days of my confinement.

The treatment that I got at first was befitting that of a super commando. That was quite a dubious honour because I was not even a commando. I protested vigorously, and by-and-by my protestations served to make my physical discomfort more bearable. However, the guards never relaxed their vigilance. I drew a number of sightseers. I imagine that my antics before I was taken prisoner must have caused quite a sensation. The Indians (and some Bengalis) were convinced that I was from the SSG (Intelligence) who had been sent to assassinate Col. Osmany. For his part Osmany was convinced that this was true—and Khaled Mosharraf cleverly played up the drama to the hilt. Col. Osmany gave orders that I should be shot. But Brig. Pande and the BSF had other ideas. I was a prized 'super commando' for them and they refused to hand me over.

The guards that were assigned to guard me while I was in custody were in civilian clothes, which was unusual. A JCO always sat next to the cell door clutching a pistol. When some time had passed, they began to chat quite amiably with me. Two of them, Haripal and Jai Singh, were quite young and as we became more informal, they began to regale me with stories of Ajmer and Amritsar.

The first interrogation team made its appearance on 6 April 1971. Thus began my long ordeal with members of this silent profession. My entire stay in 91 BSF was studded with interrogation teams, who were relentless in one solitary pursuit, i.e., information, accessing of which was their sustenance. I can write an entire book on the methods that they recourse to in order to extract information out of you. At first they resorted to flattery and coercion, and subsequently threats. But I remained unwavering as to my story, which of course happened to be the truth, and which of course they chose not to believe.

At the beginning of the interrogation and for the first two days thereafter, a few Indian BSF officers, mostly of Punjabi origin, bent the rules to come and talk to me occasionally. Capt. (or Assistant Commandant) Manna, who originally belonged to Jhelum, even brought magazines, a toothbrush and toothpaste. I gathered from their conversation that they were to be the advisors to the rebel army. It was easy to sense that for some of them the job was not particularly to their liking. I could see a constant flow of rebel leaders, political and military, going to the Officer's Mess which was hardly 150 yards away. It was like a gathering of vultures flocking to prey upon the carcass of Pakistan.

A Quarter Guard Cell is a cell, not a five-star hotel. As a soldier one can be resigned to its discomforts. However when the benign interrogation failed to achieve the desired result, the next step was obvious. Third degree methods vary: the army's method is to deliver blows to your body. One is lucky if they do not use rifle butts and it is not solely directed at your head. You may sustain internal injuries and may be rendered immobile but you are still able to sustain their pressure.

Indian Border Security Force is a para-military force somewhere in between the army and the police. They were extremely brutal. Till today I wake up in cold sweat over the torture methods they resorted to on me. Even though decades have gone by but my hatred for them has not ebbed. Needless to say I could bear the punishment for some time. Luckily for me their torture tactics began after nearly two days and only persisted for 24 hours. I was almost beyond feeling pain—it felt as if every bone in my body had been broken. I became unconscious. A person can sustain torture for a while before he breaks down, and if he is lucky he will reach a level of numbness where he will neither be able to feel pain or pleasure—a nether world of semi-consciousness and blackout. This saves him from the humiliation of being completely broken. I was beaten beyond consciousness and in that sense I consider myself lucky since I was spared the humiliation of being broken.

When I regained consciousness an argument was taking place. I was hauled up, taken out of my cell and thrown on the ground. Although it was evening, I could make out the green colour of Indian Army uniforms. After sometime I was lifted into an ambulance and taken to what seemed to be an MI Room. Slipping between consciousness and oblivion, I was aware of a doctor and nurses being present. I did not feel the prick of the injection that lulled me into a blissful sleep. When I woke up, although, I was lying on a hospital bed, I could make out that it was not a hospital. Every bone in my body was aching; my head feeling many times its size. I realized that I had been shaved and given a sponge bath while I was asleep. Outside the room I could still hear some argument carrying on but it was very subdued as compared to the one that had been going on when I was carried away from the 91 BSF cell.

From what I could gather, the Indian Army came to know that a Pakistani officer (possibly a super commando) was in the custody of 91 BSF. Obviously they wanted to interrogate me. However, when they discovered me in the state that I was in, they reported the matter to their Brigade Commander. I cannot speak with certainty but I think his name was Rawat. Whoever he might have been, he certainly proved to be my saviour. He immediately instructed the BSF to hand me over to the army but the BSF refused. As is typical of soldiers, when someone other than themselves are roughing up somebody, they take umbrage at a soldier being treated in such a brutal manner. Upon the orders of Brig. Rawat an army squad was called to 91 BSF and I was physically taken away.

However, politics is politics, and in those early days the Indian Army had still not been entrusted with the task of intervening in East Pakistan. All action at that time was in the hands of the BSF. After maybe a day or two, although, still bruised but not broken, I was able to stand. I was handed back to the BSF but not to 91 BSF. I was to be handed over to the civil authorities for further interrogation. I was later advised by an affable interrogator in Dacca not to narrate the incident of where the Indian Army had taken me after I was snatched from the Border Security Force. This would shed a negative connotation as to my intentions.

What nonsense, the devil must be given his due!

Although my brethren colleagues at the 2E Bengal spared my life but they did give me a living death. As to the reason why they did this is beyond my comprehension. We were all Pakistanis and fellow soldiers. They knew that I loved my country and harboured no ill intentions. How could they turn against me overnight? If they could not keep me in their captivity due to the contingency of operations, that could have been understandable—they should have shot and buried me on Pakistani soil—this much at least a man can expect of his brothers. But to hand me over to the enemy as hostage and let them do as they pleased with me was treachery.

I was filled with hatred for them at that time and despised each one of them for what they had done to me. But divine justice prevails: nearly all those who actively conspired against me to turn me into a captive in the hands of the enemy has suffered at the hands of their own soldiers— in the country they liberated—and that shall remain on their epitaph! What an irony of fate that Maj. Khaled Mosharraf, who later became Major General, was bayoneted and shot by soldiers belonging to 2E Bengal [most likely No. 6 Platoon B Company] in the counter-coup that brought Ziaur Rahman to power in 1975. He was caught and executed while fleeing along with others when his coup collapsed. To his credit he propped up the other two officers who were about to be executed. I believe his last words were: 'you lived like a man, now die like a man.' Although not one of my favourite people, I have no rancour against Mosharraf. Under the circumstances, he had to do what he did to me. He was a courageous soldier and the cause of his downfall was his ambition!

On the night of 11 April 1971, I was escorted from the Army MI Room by Captain Manna along with a BSF guard to Kotwali Thana, Agartala. Having undergone a detailed inspection by the Thana Sub-Inspector, I was removed to a dingy, wet cell. The smell of urine pervading in that cell was nauseating and that rag which functioned as a coverlet had to be seen to be believed. I raised quite a tantrum but to no avail. Now that I was conscious and the full brunt of my predicament hit me, this was the one day that I lost hope and sincerely wished to die. I beseeched God to either give me freedom or else death. That night was the worst night of my life. I will remember the darkness, the loneliness and the clammy chill, both within and without, for a long time to come. The memory of it sends shivers through me till today. The experience shall continue to haunt me.

My saga may be paraphrased by these memorable lines from *The Bridges of Toko Ri by* James A. Michener:

'I was now all alone at a place I did not want to be.'

NOTES

1. The period encompassing the early 1970s is a complex period. It is a history that must be recorded, but by someone truly neutral, which I believe myself to be since my mother was Bengali and father a Punjabi. If the Bengalis suffered at the hands of their Punjabi brothers (as all West Pakistanis, be they Pathan, Sindhi, Baloch etc. were called), I suffered along with them—and when conversely the West Pakistanis suffered at the hands of the Bengalis, I also suffered with them. And although after forty years this prejudice might have somewhat ebbed, it has not altogether disappeared.

2. Mohammad Ataul Ghani Osmany was born in Sunamganj, Sylhet Division, East Bengal, on 1 September 1918. He joined the Pakistan Army on 7 October 1947 as a Major and was promoted to the rank of Lieutenant Colonel. He retired as a Colonel in 1967.

   Colonel Osmany earned a reputation as a hard-nosed, stubborn officer. A legend among Bengali servicemen for his willingness to butt heads with the brass, he joined the Awami League and was elected MNA in the General Elections held in Pakistan in 1970. Failing to persuade Sheikh Mujibur Rahman to go into hiding, Osmany himself hid in Dacca [Dhaka] until 29 March 1971. He shaved off his famous moustache and made for the Indian border. Osmany was elected as Commander-in-Chief of the joint forces of Bangladesh in April 1971 by Bengali officers, a choice ratified by the Bangladeshi government-in-exile. In April 1972 he retired as the first full General of the Bangladesh Army.

2

AGARTALA JAIL

Next morning, while food was being served, I met Lieutenant Colonel Aziz Sheikh, Major Iqbal Ahmed and Captain Ayaz Mahmood. Like me, they were wet and miserable but we gained comfort in each other's presence. They were West Pakistani officers serving with East Pakistan Rifles (EPR) in Chittagong. They were taken prisoners by EPR's Major Rafique, who in fact was the first Bengali officer to raise the flag of rebellion in the Chittagong area. There is a controversy in Bangladesh that Ziaur Rahman had led the revolt in East Pakistan, which is patently not true. He was the first person to announce it on radio, but in fact it was Major Rafique who spearheaded the revolt in Chittagong. He later handed over the three officers to Maj. Ziaur Rahman in Ramgarh area. Captain Ayaz's wounds were fresh. Ten days had hardly passed since India was a shared enemy to both, East Pakistani rebels and us. We belonged to the same camaraderie of officers. Now the parting of ways had come: yesterday's friends were today's enemies; and yesterday's enemy was today a friend of our friend. Such is life, at least for those fortunate enough to have survived those days.

It was a wet and rainy day. As we were driven to the court in a jeep wagon, we were all shivering with cold. A very smart no-nonsense young sub-inspector soon received orders to confine us to Agartala Jail. In the Court House, we came in for a detailed inspection by a large number of on-lookers, including some girls. Our inspection of each other was mutual.

When we reached Agartala Jail, it loomed large in front of us, ominous and yellow. I had an advantage over others since I could speak passable Bengali. I thought that the only way to get out of here was to bluff my way out. That required me to continue posing as a genuine rebel. I was kept separately from the other Pakistani prisoners in a different block.

The desire to escape is always present. Moreover, information about the extent of Indian involvement would have been urgently required in

Pakistan. The only method to obtain freedom in such circumstances is to obtain it through all means possible and without holding back. My first stroke of luck came with my initial meeting with the Jail Warden. A kindly man, he noticed my anguish and instructed the warden leading me to Block 5 to put me under the care of Majumdar. I found out that Majumdar was a Naxalite.[1] Naxalites, Naxals or Naksalvadis are a 'Maoist communist group in India who are engaged in the Naxalite-Maoist insurgency.'

Majumdar was someone who evoked tremendous respect among prison circles—from Jail Wardens to under-trial convicts and others. Hence, Majumdar turned out to be a chieftain of sorts and also possessed the demeanour of one. Block 5 consisted of two cells containing about 20 people in each cell, including Manipuris. A mat and couple of blankets were issued to me to serve as a bed. My new friend Majumdar arranged them in such a manner so that I was placed next to him.

Friendship is a peculiar emotion—it transcends race, colour, creed and other barriers. This bearded young man (he shaved his beard later on) next to me, with the eyes of a hawk, was the perfect antithesis to me. My contention then was (and still is) that the rule of law is paramount but the Naxalites did not recognize any laws, hence, Majumdar did not feel any sense of moral guilt in breaking rules. While I adhere to the dictates of society, my new-found friend Majumdar had shunned society. He harboured absolute contempt for law-abiding and peace-loving citizens; his only fealty lay with the rule of the people. His purpose in life, he told me, was to annihilate society as it existed and then evolve a new rule of law, i.e., rule of the people based on Marxist-Leninist principles. This was to be achieved through all possible means, and if necessary, even through violence. Although I could not agree with him, yet he spoke with such disarming frankness that I could not dislike his candour either. He reached out his hand in friendship towards me without any motive, and at a time when I was in dire need of a friend. I was in a state of despair, hence, I accepted his overtures and we sub-sequently developed a bond of affinity without any strings attached. This kind of friendship is rare these days.

One of my main issues with those who debriefed me in Dacca on my return concerned my account of the Naxalites, because no one would believe me since they had heard or knew nothing about them. This was not so surprising: very little information was available about them in 1971. Even after so many decades very few know who they are.

The convicts of Agartala Jail 'ruled the roost', as the saying goes, behaving like true, lawless citizens of any state. Inside the walls of the prison, they were a law within the law and they exercised their prerogatives with cruel and absolute authority. They were responsible to the wardens for the discipline of the rest of the inmates, a curious situation which they exploited to their advantage.

How is one supposed to feel when a murderer or a rapist is given the authority of monitoring one's cell in the prison and is lecturing others on 'good conduct and behaviour'? They were sadists and behave as such, but fortunately none of it was practiced on me. The convicts were brutal with the rest of the inmates in the interpretation of their particular law. I was counselled by Majumdar to display patience and fortitude.

The Naxalities were a different lot altogether. They did not exercise authority over anyone but at the same time did not allow anyone to exercise any sort of authority over them: neither the prison staff nor the convicts. They were simply left alone and treated with marked respect. In turn they left everyone else alone. They were scattered in different cells in twos and threes. But besides the fact that they were behind bars, they otherwise were quite free to do as they desired. I found later that they did not even bother to protest their captivity. I was lucky to have been adopted by Majumdar, known as 'MA' to his friends, and kept safe under his wing. He had thrown a protective mantle over me from the murderous designs of the convicts, who were impatient to tear me to pieces. Once, while noticing the jailor speak to him with marked deference, I did venture to ask Majumdar his trade secret. Majumdar gave me a wry smile, and said sardonically: 'he has a son.' The meaning manifest in those words was eloquent enough to me. In the law of the jungle, the threat of swift, devastating reaction can become quite ominous. I can understand why they never took their pleas to law courts—they simply did not recognize the law.

The other major group of persons held in detention without trial were from Manipur.[2] They were quite young, between the ages of 18 and 20, and had been in prison for the last two years. Some of these Manipuris also became quite friendly with me. As much as I could gather from their animated conversation, they belonged to the more affluent and influential Masyarins who constituted the elite among Manipuris and were being held as hostage by India in sufferance for good behaviour by their families in Manipur. The rest were a motley crew belonging to the general category of under-trials. They had all had been slapped with ad-hoc charges on some obscure count of the Indian

Law. Some of them were imprisoned for genuine crimes, while some had been thrown behind bars for having incurred the displeasure of one of the law enforcement agencies of India and were languishing in Agartala Jail awaiting their trial. Such are the vagaries of the 'benign' Indian Law—and the situation is no different in Pakistan or Bangladesh.

Until I reached the precincts of Agartala Jail, I never realized the haughty 'Prussian Army Officer' mindset I had developed. I pride myself on sleeping on the ground, eating and fighting along with my soldiers which is the way of all officers of the army—but to degrade myself to the level of convicts was a little too much. But I learnt many lessons there. Some of these pertained to discretion and humility although these were not knocked into me because of divine providence but through the bitter experiences that I suffered. When man is stripped of all dignity, the only asset that is left is pride and honour, and if one is to give one's life for it, then so be it.

The first time I was given food, the tin plate in which it was slopped in was literally thrown at my feet. I did not touch the food and went and crouched in a corner. The rage and disgust that I felt at the time cannot be elucidated in words. As I sat there, a young short, tough convict with unruly hair came up to me with another tin plate of food. With an obviously nasal Punjabi accent, he quietly prodded me to eat the food. He told me that he too was a Pakistani soldier and it was the duty of a soldier to bring food for their officers with their own hands. I was overwhelmed with emotion. My pride was mingled with shame since as Muslims we are never to turn food away.

This young soldier's name was Khaliq. He was an artillery soldier hailing from Dina in the Jhelum district. While he was posted in Mainamati Cantonment near Comilla, he had been caught at the border in unfortunate circumstances two-and-a-half years ago. He suffered from endless misfortune since the Indians would release him and then would re-arrest him on some pretext or the other and convict him. I cannot express in words how Khaliq took care of me for the remainder of my sojourn at Agartala Jail. He appointed himself as my batman and guardian of sorts. I feel great sorrow at the fact that it should have been me, by virtue of being an officer, who should have been taking care of him rather than him being my support. Although he was in a pathetic condition but was bearing up cheerfully and manfully. Because of our sudden departure from the jail, I could not even bid him goodbye. One of my great regrets in life is that I do not know what eventually became of him.

Majumdar the Naxalite possessed a chessboard and he and others took turns to play with me, crushing my pride in my prowess in the game to pulp. He also had a number of books and a few very old copies of the *Reader's Digest* which I read over and over again. Since my Bengali was not fluent enough to pass a critical appraisal, I desisted from speaking it as much as I could.

It was approximately middle of April 1971 that Captain Amin Choudhry was also brought to the same block. He belonged to the 4th Battalion of the East Bengal Regiment. His arrival was good for me for two reasons. Firstly, because it diverted the immediate attention of all concerned from me, and secondly, because it afforded me some company of my kind. Amin remained wary of me at first because he was a Bengali and a professional rebel, whereas, I was a Pakistani calling myself a rebel. He was also quite exhausted by the release of emotions but he lost no time in settling down and establishing workable relations with the powers that were. The general convicts and the Naxalites both warmed up to him immediately. But the Manipuris remained averse to him because of their prejudice against Bengalis.

Amin and I were poles apart in our ideas and philosophies. But like Majumdar, we gradually thawed towards each other and afterwards got on quite well. I could not agree with Amin's views as regards the disintegration of nationhood, but he disagreed with me without any rancour. I agreed with him that the way the units of the East Bengal Regiment were being treated in East Pakistan, they were left with no other option but to revolt in anticipation of being disarmed. While it is true that the planning among a core of Bengali officers was done with meticulous care, 2E Bengal revolted only after they heard what had happened to 1E Bengal in Jessore. I have great respect for Amin as a friend. He was never rude or impolite even though I provided him with enough provocation at times.

A person must possess the moral courage to speak his beliefs out aloud and also own up to his weaknesses. Amin possessed a lot of moral courage for which I admire him greatly. There were numerous mutual topics that we discussed in jail which served as a neutral ground for us. Although because of the prevailing circumstances our goals had become different. However at this stage I could not openly rebut him on salient points but focus primarily on the moral aspect of the issue. Nevertheless, I could never think of Amin as my enemy.

A herd of Pakistanis followed Amin into the Agartatla Jail. At first the arrivals were restricted to non-Bengalis but then Pakistanis of

Bengali origin started pouring in. I later read a statement by so-called responsible Indian readers that 5 per cent of the rogues pouring in from Pakistan were agent provocateurs and saboteurs. Since India was claiming that 7 million refugees had crossed over into India, the number works out to be a stupendous 350,000. So much for their 'intelligence'!

Two tea planters, Abid Hussain and Allauddin Siddiky were the first to arrive in our block. They were accompanied by their families who were taken to the women's block, including Abid Hussain's eighty-year-old mother. One could only imagine their distress, although, both were displaying immense fortitude and possessed a cheerful disposition and were therefore pleasant company. Then Asmat Shah was brought in and the quorum was complete. Asmat, the brother of Major Raza Shaheed, happened to be a school buddy of mine from Lawrence College days. We Ghoragali boys can get together in any adversity and produce humour which is our particular trademark. Moreover, Asmat and I had been involved in many escapades together in school. The social life in Agartala Jail was showing an upward trend.

What does one do in such circumstances? Does one resign oneself to one's fate or lead a day-to-day existence with positive spirits. The answer would be somewhere in the middle although under such conditions the mood can vary from elation to absolute despair. The only attributes that one can cling to are pride and dignity.

The tea planters in British companies that were based in Calcutta were trying to obtain the release of Abid Hussain and Allauddin Siddiky. A James Finaly was sent to the jail by the company to serve as a representative for negotiations regarding Abid and Siddiky's release. He had brought money and parcels of daily necessities for them, and the prospect of their release seemed bright. By this time there was a continuous inflow of other tea planters from the Sylhet area, some with large families including expectant mothers. It was therefore not unreasonable to expect that the Indian Government would not take too much time in releasing them. I was happy for them. Under all the banter and jovialness that they were displaying, the ones whose families had also been made captives along with them were feeling the pinch. They were feeling sorry for me since they realized that it would be sometime before somebody bestowed their benevolence upon me. But all of us had overestimated Indian benevolence and humanity. These people were still languishing in jail even when I had reached Pakistan.

I tried my best to brief Asmat and Ali on information that was important to make a getaway. They would memorize their 'lessons' everyday. It was quite a game. In order to bolster their sagging morale, I would conjure up a favourable strategic picture of Pakistan in case of war with India even though I well knew that the odds were against us. Such was my enthusiasm. I fear that I was soon considered a 'war lover' by them. However, through my arguments, their morale got a tremendous boost. Amin naturally did not subscribe to these feelings. And had he been antagonistic towards me, my views would have been fatal for me. But after having lived with Amin for sometime, I came to understand the level of his loyalty towards a friend or a superior, but at that time I could not take such a risk with him.

My mind was already evaluating ways and means of affecting an escape. Through observation and interaction I had learnt a lot about the layout and routine of Agartala Jail. The requisite gaps were filled in by Khaliq. The sound of Pakistani Artillery targeting the Mukti Bahini in adjacent Pakistani territory was clearly audible, Akhaura being not more than four miles away. Later on, even the jail would reverberate from the sounds. A desperate scheme had already half formed in my mind. However when I spoke to Asmat Shah, he appraised me of certain drawbacks even if the plan were totally successful. The retaliation on the families and remaining Pakistanis would have been swift and vengeful. We decided it was not worth the risk.

The tea planters would meet their families occasionally and I kept badgering them to find out if any women and children had been brought from Chittagong. I had heard that the rebels had captured a few as hostages and I desperately wanted to hear of some news about my cousins who lived in the area where one of the rebel battalions had been located. However Abid and Ali every time came back with the news that no families had been brought from Chittagong. When I returned to Pakistan later, I came to know the details of murder, arson, loot and rape that were perpetrated on the people of Chittagong in the name of 'freedom'. I knew a lot of families in Chittagong. The blood of those innocents and the tortures that were inflicted on them is a display of the cruelty of those who were privileged to once wear the uniform as soldiers. When soldiers make war on women and children, they cease to be soldiers. That is why in the final analysis, when it came to real combat, they could not face up to bullets which is their actual job as soldiers. It is sickening to even remember that I once served with some of these men and feel disappointed, disillusioned, and progressively disgusted, that I had such faith and confidence in them. What sort of men were they that they could inflict such cruelties on helpless beings?

They may have forgotten their oaths of fealty, but could they forget that they were also human beings? Unfortunately, the same may be said of the Pakistan Army. The terror that was unleashed by them in East Pakistan between March and November 1971 is simply inexcusable.

Coming back to Agartala Jail. We were privileged to see one movie titled: *Nai Roshni* which had Mala Sinha and Ashok Kumar as lead actors. Both of them performed excellently. Since I do not mind Indian films at all, Agartala Jail was beginning to become bearable.

But all good things must come to an end.

I possess a sizable amount of self control except when it concerns my pride and honour. When these are attacked, I lose control quickly and violently. Some demon inside me comes to life which I am not able to control—and for this I have suffered much. The other aspect of my personality that I have trouble with is my high level of allergy for certain types of people. I very occasionally run into somebody who begins to irritate me for no rhyme or reason. I lose my control much in the same manner as mentioned above, at times with unfortunate consequences.

There was a particular convict who happened to be the monitor of our cell. He was a convicted rapist and his lewd jokes would grate on my nerves. My level of irritation towards him gradually increased. Although he had not dared to attack me directly because of Majumdar, I could sense his antagonism along with some other convicts towards me. I had fallen from their grace due to my 'haughty' attitude. Moreover, I had encountered most of the Pakistani civilians that had been brought in as prisoners at some point in time. In an alien country and locked up in the unfriendly atmosphere of the jail, they were beginning to realize the value of peace and tranquillity that once prevailed in their country. As an army officer, I became a natural candidate as their guide and mentor. How was I to console them except by telling them to show faith and perseverance and pray for the unity of our country? Their display of deference towards me was noticed by the jail hierarchy who decided to cut me down to size. Majumdar had warned me about any retaliatory reaction on my part and advised me to display fortitude even if I was provoked to the extreme, as this would result in the cessation of Majumdar's protective mantle over me. Thus I was trying to control myself as much as was within my power but the rapist would try my patience to the limits. I began to abhor his mere sight. Once, when he hurled an insult towards me, I lost my self control and disregarding all advice reacted in an extreme manner. It required Amin, Abid and Asmat to hold me down. This action of mine was enough to stir up quite a hornet's nest. The warders were approached by the monitor who whined away my misdeeds to them. I was seething with anger and would have retaliated further had Ali and Asmat not calmed me down. Better sense subsequently prevailed over me and I meekly submitted to being removed to another block but in the same compound, where there was an unholy preponderance of convicts.

During the next few days, it was God who kept my pride and honour intact. Many times I was provoked into situations where my patience was tried to the utmost. It was a day-to-day survival for me in Block 4. The prison grapevine had informed the other inmates of this block of my 'crime' for which I was to be punished. However, Khaliq who was also in the same cell with me along with 90 other convicts literally forced me to show perseverance. He must have also spoken to my adversaries in the cell because, apart from ferocious glares from them, I was by and large left alone to brood over my misdemeanours in isolation.

Block 4 was inhabited by a large number of Manipuris. When the convicts were out for their work drill, we were left alone to chat with each other. They took pains in providing me details about their Manipuri language and Meitei religion and wanted to know about Pakistan. Hence there was much exchange of views as regards our respective countries. Despite my protestations, they did not for a moment believe that I was a rebel. How can I ever forget people like Biren, Manihar, Mahez, Shanayam, Chitharaekh and Shyam Kumar?

Matters settled down after a couple of days although I remained in the same cell. The cell was crawling with numerous characters—I also witnessed some vicious beatings that were inflicted on newcomers. There were a couple of tea planters here also and we kept company from time to time—coming together in our misfortune. I could talk to my other comrades whenever the cell doors were opened. Since I was not in possession of even a single 'naya paisa', they would take turns in treating me at the canteen. During this time, I recalled all the rules that we would break at Lawrence College. Agartala Jail was indeed a strange meeting place.

I had to undergo further interrogation by the Border Security Force (BSF) and Police teams. They were a nuisance, especially the BSF team, since the Captain interrogating me was obviously inexperienced but dogged in his persistence to obtain any information. The Police team was fun—they were thoroughly confused by my tale and I was enjoying myself and confusing them further with my aeronautical and technical jargon. Hence, they gave up on me. Interrogation can also work both ways. Through their questioning I had managed to glean some information about the world outside. Fair amount of information was also provided by the prison grapevine. Hence, we were quite well-informed about the course of events.

During this time, another man from the realm of intelligence made his presence known. He called himself Lt. Col. Menon and was a very intelligent and incisive man. He spent the first day of interrogation going into my personal history and events leading up to the current date. Next day he widened the horizon of his interrogation and asked questions pertaining to military and strategic matters. I was agog at his questions and told him so!

Col. Memon was a sophisticated individual and though he insisted he was from the BSF, his demeanour and techniques labelled him from the army, or ex-army serving with the Intelligence Bureau (IB) or RAW. He went into painstaking details over every issue, but was never threatening or rude. He told me that he was an amateur palmist and asked me if he could read my palm. After gazing at my palm for some time, he gave me a quizzical look. He said he could not understand something—if my story of having joined my unit 2E Bengal in good faith was true—then my career was over. But then, he said, how is it that my career line [in the army] is unbroken for a few more years? He also told me that I would also be very successful but only after going through a considerable period of hardship and struggle. He declared that what he read in the lines of my palm did not make sense and that there was certainly something amiss in my story and what the stars were foretelling. Thereafter he seemed to change his tack considerably but I stuck to my story, most of which was in any case truthful.

When Majumdar sat down with me one evening I could sense from his demeanour that he had something important to say to me. I soon found out what it was. He had received information through the prison grapevine and other sources that we were going to be shifted to Calcutta—most likely to Fort William—in the next few days. It could even be the next day. He immediately began to coach me about places in Calcutta and its vicinity. He continued to hammer information into me until I had completely memorized it. Interestingly, he often spoke about a town by the name of Burdwan. And much later, when the Indians traced me back to my connection with Majumdar, they began to look for me in Naxal safe havens. Over the next few days I realized something else, Majumdar really did care for my welfare. Or was I a target for recruitment? Maybe the Naxalites felt that this was an opportunity to have someone in their ranks who possessed a trained military mind!

In all I had spent approximately three weeks in Agartala Jail. The fact that I had experienced the confines of a prison—that too an Indian one—was an experience in itself. It is not a pleasant remembrance. However it must be stated that the exposure to the variety of humankind incarcerated behind the prison walls, with no holds barred, was a complete experience in itself.

I was lucky to have escaped the long-term scars of my experiences at the Agartala Jail.

NOTES

1. Even now people have scarce knowledge about the Naxalites. The name 'Naxalite' is derived from 'Naxalbari', a village situated in West Bengal where the movement originated. A section of the Communist Party of India led by Charu Majumdar, Kanu Sanyal and Jangal Santhal initiated a violent uprising in 1967. Considered as far-left radicals, the Naxals are supportive of the Maoist political sentiment and ideology.

   Inspired by the doctrines of Mao Zedong, Charu Majumdar provided ideological leadership for the Naxalbari movement. He advocated that Indian peasants and lower caste tribals overthrow the government and the upper caste class by force. The ideology spread through Charu Majumdar's writings which also attracted a large number of urban elite. His historic 'Eight Documents' formed the basis of the Naxalite ideology.

   Practically all Naxalite factions trace their origin to the Communist Party of India (Marxist-Leninist). The movement was initially centred in West Bengal but they covertly spread their activities into less developed areas of rural central and eastern India, such as Bihar, Chhattisgarh, Orissa and Andhra Pradesh. Violent uprisings were organized in several parts of the country The Naxalites gained a strong presence amongst radical students of Calcutta. They advocated [armed] resistance to 'class enemies': the landlords, university teachers, police personnel, politicians and others in seats of power and influence. The Naxalites took over the Jadavpur University, making their headquarters in the Presidency College, Calcutta [Kolkata]. Some of the educated elite from other educational institutions of India also supported them.

   The Naxalites alleged human rights violations by the West Bengal police who responded that the state was effectively fighting a civil war with them. In 1972 Majumdar was arrested by the police and died in Alipore Jail. His death accelerated the fragmentation of the movement.

   Naxalites are considered as prime 'terrorists' of India. They are active in approximately 220 districts of 20 states. According to RAW (Research and Analysis Wing), 20,000 armed Naxalites are operating in the field in addition to 50,000 regular cadres. Their growing influence prompted Indian Prime Minister

Manmohan Singh to declare them to be the most serious internal threat to India's national security.

2. Bounded by the Indian states of Nagaland to the north, Mizoram to the south and Assam to the west, Manipur is a state in north-eastern India. Its capital is Imphal. Rangoon [Myanmar] borders it to the east. The Meiteis form the primary ethnic group and their language is known as Manipuri. Manipur is still considered by Indians as a sensitive border state. In 1890 the Maharaja of Manipur, Surya Chandra Singh, was overthrown by his two younger brothers. He pleaded protection from the British Political Agent, F.C. Grimwood, abdicated, and left the State of Manipur. The new rulers of Manipur remained at odds with the British which resulted in a battle of sorts between the two. Manupuris murdered the Chief Commissioner of Assam, Grimwood, and three army officers. The British forces from Assam and Burma managed to control the uprising and Manipur came under British control.

Due to missionary activity, particularly by the Baptists, Christians constitute 34 per cent of the population of Manipur. Foreigners till today are not allowed in the Manipur state without a Restricted Area Permit.

3

PASSAGE TO PANAGARH

A few minutes before we were taken from Agartala Jail to Agartala Airport by a mixed escort of the Border Security Force (BSF) and the Police, I met up with the rest of the Pakistan Army officers who were in incarceration. Lt. Col. Khizar Hayat was Commanding officer (CO) 4E Bengal, and Major Sadiq Nawaz was originally from Engineers but after joining the SSG was transferred to infantry (and to the Bengal Regiment). He was a Company Commander in 4E Bengal. Lt. Amjad Saeed was the Intelligence Officer (IO) to the CO. I knew Col. Khizar Hayat since I was five years old. He had come to 2E Bengal in Jessore as a Second Lieutenant and to me he had always been an 'uncle'. He possessed a stoic, fatherly demeanour. He was not really considered outstanding in his profession, therefore, it was a bonus for him to be assigned the command of an infantry unit. I did not know Major Sadiq Nawaz well even though I was acquainted with him because of the close contact between Army Aviation and the SSG. It was the first time that I was meeting Lt. Amjad Saeed.

A man who is a prisoner in a hostile country does not have a choice in any matter. His only option is to follow the dictates that stem from the prodding of a bayonet.

On the morning of 30 April 1971, we were rid of Agartala Jail for good. Our departure was without much ceremony except for the customary blindfolding. For good measure our hands were also tied behind our backs. The few glimpses that we would occasionally manage to capture through our blindfold were of a large, curious crowd gaping at us. Ten of us, all Pakistanis, were bundled into an Indian-made Mercedes Benz truck. We were not really mishandled, but at the same time we were not treated with much tact either. We were piled up along with our bedrolls and luggage. A neat bit of packing by our escort! It is part of the psyche of military men to do map reading. Hardly had we taken a turn or two when Major Sadiq Nawaz whispered to me that we must be heading for the airport. I was inclined to agree but was feeling too elated and safe among my own kind to really care. While we were at Agartala Jail we could hear the sound of Pakistani artillery pounding at Mukti Bahini positions near the adjacent border. This would naturally send tremors through the jail and also through the nerves of the convicts and other inmates and our entente cordiale with them. The edge of Agartala Airport runway nearly touched the Pakistan border next to Akhaura Railway Junction. From Akhaura the railway line coming from Chittagong through Comilla continues through the tea estates adjacent to the border to Sylhet. The other line forks northwest through Brahmanbaria, then to Bhairab Bazaar and Narsingdi before continuing on to Mymensingh through Kishoreganj. Another line branches off through Tongi to Dacca.

As a commercial airfield Agartala had daily Indian Airlines flights to Calcutta circling the northern part of East Pakistan, passing over Shillong and Darjeeling. Agartala also had both, fixed and helicopter aircraft of the Indian Air Force. Flying many times adjacent to the border one could make out Dakotas and the odd Alouette-3. Since the airfield did not possess any real defence, it would have been very easy for the Pakistani military to capture it. I could never imagine that I would one day be passing through this airfield as a prisoner. We were brought to the airfield blindfolded and without any clue as to where we were being taken. Through the grapevine, Majumdar had told me that it was believed we would be taken to HQ's Indian Eastern Command at Fort William in Calcutta. He told us that Naxalites were very active in the area, especially in and around the town of Burdwan which was situated approximately 100 hours west of Calcutta.

Once at the airfield, we could make out, again by effectively peeping through our blindfolds that a Fokker Friendship aircraft, an MI-4 Helicopter and a Dakota awaited our arrival. We soon gave up all hopes of being transported in the Indian Airlines Fokker—the Indians would never allow us the luxury of being served by airhostesses. It was a pleasurable thought though. The MI-4 Helicopter was not chosen to be our airborne chariot, also, since our numbers inclusive of our escort exceeded over twenty. I myself did not particularly mind; the MI-4 (in the Pakistani inventory we had the more versatile MI-8) is not the best among helicopters.

We were hauled off the trucks and led onto the steps leading into the jeep of the aircraft, the evergreen Dakota. As I stumbled into the World War II vintage aircraft, I remembered that it had been a long long time that I had last seen a Dakota. It had been obsolete in Pakistan for a while although the sight of one brings back pleasant memories of our country that once was.

Putting our life in the hands of God and wishing against hope that the pilot knew his business, we acquired seats with our backs to the windows. A peculiar phenomenon exists which applies to all pilots anywhere. A pilot is never ever confident as a passenger, even if the aeroplane is being flown by his most trusted friend unless he has utter confidence in his flying abilities, which is rare. Anyway, there we were: Pakistanis all bound together on the right side of the aircraft. Sitting across us, in proper order and with eyes wide open were 10 Indian soldiers in jungle green uniform, having the shoulder title of the Bihar Regiment, and clutching tightly to their Indian-made sub-machine guns (SMG) with collapsible butts. Their excitement as custodians of live Pakistani soldiers, and that too mostly officers was so obviously electric that it engulfed you with the need for caution, lest one of us should sneeze suddenly and start off an unwholesome chain reaction. Their Captain, as befits a person of his rank, was trying to appear unconcerned and indifferent. He was emanating a haughty demeanour, as if escorting Pakistani prisoners was an everyday occurrence to him. Through the slits of our blindfold we were able to see him, and what is more, he knew that we could see him. He remained next to the opening for the door itself was non-existent.

There was a pleasant interlude before our journey began. There seemed to be an inordinate delay and it became unbearably hot. Lt. Col. Khizer Hayat, the senior-most officer among us, had been commissioned into the Pakistan Army but strictly followed the dictates of the old British Indian Army. His principle of life was very simple: trust in Almighty God and obey all commands given to you by whoever was in authority over you without question. It compels us to believe that this worthy scion of an older generation did not reason in his mind the validity of our captivity and thus our blindfolds. To him it was an edict by authorities concerned and therefore to be obeyed. He therefore chose not to see what the other rather undisciplined members of a newer generation were already aware of: that we were in an aircraft. Or was he in his own way attempting a deception plan? The weather being sultry, the good Colonel ventured past his natural reserve of manner and requested the sentry nearest to him in a quavering voice if he could kindly lift the tarpaulin of the truck. I am afraid that the Indians did not see much humour in our sudden burst of laughter—even the Colonel seemed aggrieved. The Indians grew more wary, clutched their weapons with greater devotion and cast hostile glances at us. Their thought at that point must have been: 'What manner of men (or monsters) were these who saw fit to laugh in such dangerous circumstances?'

We Pakistanis are a funny lot. We usually underestimate each other until we find ourselves on a particularly sticky wicket—it is only then that the best that is within us asserts itself, and we achieve brilliant results. Only then are we convinced that we were capable of success. This makes us very unpredictable—it also results in our enemies to be wary of us. Our confidence in ourselves is supreme, whether as individuals or as a nation. A burst of humour under adverse circumstances is only a reflection of our trait as a freedom-loving people of a fighting nation.

Major Sadiq Nawaz began with our escape plans as soon as the aircraft took off. We had hardly levelled off when he began to nudge me enquiring which direction we were headed for. The position of the sun and shadow adequately defined our path to be east-by-north-east. It was safe to assess that we were heading towards Assam since whenever an Indian aircraft took off from Agartala it was invariably headed towards Assam. I casually expressed my wish that if we continued in the same direction we might hit our friendly country China.

In the meantime, Flight Lieutenant Majumdar of the Indian Air Force (IAF) who was taking a breather from flying and was engaged in good Samaritan work of passing water around to the thirsty, stumbled over my zippered boots in the process, thereby, coming to know that I was a pilot. As soon as he conveniently could, he came and squeezed himself between me and Amin. Majumdar was extremely curious to know how a pilot had landed in such circumstances and I was curious, in return, to find out where we were heading. Hence I decided to trade gossip for orientation. Once we had established a rapport we got along famously. He loosened my blindfolds slightly—in return I allowed him a little more space on the seat. When he found out that I partially belonged to the town of Bogra in East Pakistan, we got along even better and began to chat amiably. It turned out that he belonged to Pabna which is right next to the Bogra district. He was in a transport squadron based in Silchar and had been operating as a pilot in the Indian operational area (Nagaland, Mizoland and Manipur) for the last two years. He had been posted to some peace station which was why he was also carrying his scooter along with him. I asked Majumdar very innocently whether we were going to Calcutta? He said that he could not divulge this information but it was neither Calcutta nor Delhi, and that it was going to be a fairly long flight.

We had taken off around 10 am and by 10.30 am Major Sadiq Nawaz's erstwhile brain had etched out a provisional plan for our escape. Captain Amin, the only purely Bengali-origin officer was sitting in a very sombre manner between the two of us. Only one soldier who was sitting opposite us and who was despatched to keep guard over us had a sten gun with magazines in it. The weather, the scenery and the antics of the pilot had claimed the attention of our escort. Even our worthy watcher was showing signs of waning interest in us—this in turn aroused our interest. Since boarding the aircraft we had been continuously trying to loosen the grip of the ropes tied around our wrists and it was only a matter of time when our hands would become free. Sadiq and I kept updating each other with the progress. Poor Amin was sitting wedged in between us two plotters and not feeling particularly chirpy since Sadiq and I had to lean over his shoulders to talk to each other. He also did not seem pleased at the course of direction that our conversation was taking.

Our escape plan required that we loosen our ropes, jump on the soldier with the loaded weapon, and get hold of the right people concerned. We were almost free of the grip around our wrists when the Wing Commander himself, taking a breather from piloting, strolled in. He had either had an intuition or he was not comfortable with the loaded weapons, because he ordered that magazines from all weapons should be removed. Back went the magazines into the pouch—and with it our chances of freedom.

Hence we settled back into pumping Majumdar for more information. Majumdar had come back from his round at the controls and we resumed with our discourse. He laid bare his heart regarding the situation that was prevailing in East Pakistan. I could barely keep up with his monologue through the nodding of my head. He even went and fetched a newspaper to show me the latest news. He was obsessed by the Pakistan Air Force (PAF) which also seemed to be his favourite nightmare. I happily prodded him along. The captain of the Bihar Regiment was not at all amused by our chit-chat but we continued to natter away with abandon. He kept shooting venomous looks towards us but we did not care.

The process of going to the bathroom involved a minor operation in as far as the guards were concerned. It involved a precarious walk to the tail of the Dakota with tied up and blindfolded prisoners and then a gasping awareness of a gush of air coming through an open door. One's chagrin at discovering that the toilet has no outlet, or even water for that matter, has no limits when it is a long flight. When we were somewhere close to Darjeeling, Majumdar privileged me by taking off my blindfold for a good look around. By this time, the weather had really deteriorated and the aircraft was as bumpy as a camel on a wild jaunt across the desert. Being a pilot I was quite used to it and so were some of my buddies.

At approximately 3 pm on 30 April 1971 we bumped down on the tarmac of an airfield, the name of which seemed to be Indian Army's most closely guarded secret. Being insincere to them, we managed a peek anyway. On the terminal building it was written in bold black letters that it was the Panagarh Civil Airport. Although it was sunny when we landed, it soon began to rain. The Dakota took off without anyone bidding us further adieu. Majumdar, my friend of a few hours was gone.

We were piled into an ambulance belonging to the airfield. Shortly after, another Dakota landed due to bad weather. The ambulance driver who was a civilian told us that Panagarh was used as an alternate airfield. He also told us that we were eight or nine miles away from our particular destination. He said all this in a marked Bihari accent from which we concluded, wrongly of course, that we were in Bihar.

In keeping with the efficiency, spit and polish of the Indian Army, the transport assigned as our conveyance for our destination unknown was late by a full three hours. Wet and hungry, we had no fear of the unknown—nothing could have been worse than Agartala Jail. Hence we were looking forward to it with assurance. Around 6 pm some trucks finally made their belated appearance and we were bundled in. We hopelessly attempted to keep some sense of the direction we were heading in. By now it was quite dark and was increasingly becoming darker. Sounds of railway shunting could be heard. Our last sanguine thought before we reached the confines of our prison was that we may be taken somewhere farther in the train—maybe all the way to Ferozepur. Man certainly never gives up hope!

It is easy to treat such a subject with levity after the episode is over. It is galling to be a prisoner in a hostile country especially when a war has not been declared officially and you are at the mercy of your captors who may treat you as they wish. The future is always bleak, the past unbelievable, and though one may try otherwise, unforgettable. You hear only the news that the enemy wishes you to hear, which is invariably negative. And although one knows that such news is usually always bogus, in moments of sheer anguish the hopelessness inside you builds up.

Agartala Jail had been an eye-opener of how officer level prisoners were treated by the Indians. Their degradation was quite deliberate. We had been made to sleep on the floor in dingy and dirty cells—what they thought was food was slopped in front of us. The courtesy accorded to rank and which should have been accorded to us (with or without the Geneva Convention) was never observed by them at any stage. One Pakistani officer, Lieutenant Amjad Saeed had to undergo a terrible beating at the hands of warders and convicts for responding to the questions of some foreign news reporters with gusto and spirit. This being labelled as offensive behaviour, the third degree inflicted on him left the scars of sticks and clubs on him—leaving a symbolic mark on all of us. It confirmed the level of our stature in Indian eyes—we were non-entities—somewhere between the exalted position of convicts and the lowly status of under-trial prisoners. As soldiers, one could expect honourable treatment at the hands of soldiers anywhere, especially since we could not be held accountable for having fought against them, or even worse, having killed any Indian soldier at the time.

On 30 April 1971, at about 7 pm an indifferent and stoic bunch of prisoners were hauled off the trucks and made to stand in the rain while the Indians completed their 'prisoner in custody' drill according to the book. After the formalities were completed we were led into a shed where there seemed to be an unusual amount of hustle and bustle. Although our blindfolds were still bound, we still managed to take an occasional peek. As soon as our Bihar Regiment escorts had handed us over to our new captors our hands were untied and our blindfolds removed. What we saw confirmed our fears—this was to be our abode, and seemed that it would be so for a while. We found ourselves standing in front of two desks: one occupied by a Major and the other by a Lieutenant. Both were Sikhs and they were engaged in jotting down our particulars. On our right we could see a temporary 'kote' (armoury) and in the shed beyond [there were two adjacent sheds with no partition in between] we could see that on the extreme left there were some civilians, very obviously Military Engineering Services type, with another Sikh fiddling with a board containing light switches and junction boxes. We could not really see the farther shed towards our right since it was covered by a canvas partition followed by tin enclosures. We found out later that these would function as the Camp

Offices. All we could do at the time was to exchange Sikh jokes with each other.

While we had not yet quite finished giving our particulars to the two officers, in walked a gentleman wearing red tabs and with a rank of Brigadier, followed closely by another Sikh Major wearing the regalia of a military policeman. From his name badge, we gathered that the Brigadier's name was Coelho and he seemed to be beside himself with joy at seeing his charges. Coelho was real earnest in proving that Indians were not barbarous to their captives as 'we Pakistanis were'. He accused us of having mistreated Indian POWs who were captured by us during the 1965 War.

Brig. Coelho introduced the Sikh, Major R.S. Uppal, who was to be our Camp Commandant, informing us that if we had any complaints, they must be registered through him. Coelho told us that he was the Station Commander of that area, (he was wearing a helio-belt with an Artillery Crest on it and a shoulder flash sign of a Tiger emblazoned on red background). He audibly [for our benefit] gave orders to Major Uppal that the sanctioned money should be used for providing us with material comfort. Somewhat flabbergasted, Major Uppal obediently nodded.

Coelho seemed very glad to see us. Getting carried away, he announced that this was not the first instance he was coming into contact with the Pakistani POWs. He claimed that he had been engaged in the capture of Pakistani paratroopers that had been airdropped in the Pathankot Airfield area during the 1965 War. He told us that we were in his custody due to the fortunes of war and that we would be treated like officers [news to us] until we behaved otherwise. He made us understand the wide latitude that the word 'behaviour' covered. But he assured us that he would try and provide us with all the facilities available under the circumstances—books, magazines, chessboard, cards etc., and that our sojourn would be made as comfortable as possible depending, however, on how we behaved.

Coelho finally left us with the warning: 'no monkey tricks!'

4

INMATES OF PANAGARH

During the Second World War Panagarh Airport was used as a supply transport airfield by the United States Army. The airport was also used as a repair and maintenance depot by Air Technical Service Command. A squadron of B 24 Bombers covering the Burma Front operated from Panagarh in 1943.

We were informed by our captors that Panagarh[1] was known for its snakes. From the vast number of them that we came across during our stay, we had no reason to doubt them. All sizes of snakes were seen slithering over the prison. Snakes can be very elusive—it is extremely difficult to deliver a 'coup de grace' to these slimy creatures. But we did manage to kill a few of them.

The conditions that existed at the Panagarh Prison probably exist in all such prisons. One is thrown together with a varied range of individuals. Deep friendships are formed—and at the same time deep hatreds also. Each individual reacts differently to adversity—the best and the worst in them comes to the surface. Hence a person's true nature is exposed. It makes an interesting study in such situations to observe the peculiar traits of individuals that distinguishes them from each other. In such an environment, even a cursory examination of personalities provides one with a fair assessment.

The evening that we landed in Panagarh, we met the youngest among us. Second Lieutenant Syed Attaullah Shah had been brought there a few days earlier. A subaltern from 27 Baluch Regiment,[2] Shah thought at that time that he was the only survivor. His Delta Company had been deployed in Kushtia in East Pakistan, an isolated and remote town, for Internal Security (IS) duties. This was at the time when Pakistan Army's crackdown on the Bengali insurgents had begun in Dacca [end of March 1971] which led to the subsequent revolt of the East Pakistan Rifles (EPR) and police personnel, followed by the regular troops of the East Bengal Regiment. They had been taken by surprise by a sudden onslaught of combined EPR, police, and other anti-state elements. They had fought back and had tried to defend themselves as best as they could. In the process they had exhausted a negligible stock of first-line ammunition that they were carrying. Major Shoaib, the Company Commander, had tried to lead his men in a desperate attempt at a breakaway from the ring of death that was fast enclosing upon them. In the chaos and confusion of the ongoing battle, the Company had disintegrated. They were split up and separated from each other. Some had been captured alive but most had been killed. Shah had the horror of witnessing one of his fellow officers slaughtered like a sacrificial lamb by the wayside. The nightmare of this gruesome spectacle will probably haunt Shah all his life.

Since 27 Baluch Regiment had been a sister unit to 2E Bengal in 106 Brigade in Lahore in 1966–68, hence, I knew most of the officers and personnel. Shah's narration of his miraculous escape from death kept us spellbound the first few nights at the prison camp. The wounds inflicted on him were still fresh on his person. Our hearts reached out to him. As soon as he had related his experience to us, we began to retrieve whatever information we could get from him which would be helpful in our future plans of escape.

Shah had been brought to the camp from Calcutta in a jeep. This information confirmed to us that the place indeed was Panagarh. Quite observant about the route, he remembered the number of check-posts on the road. Interestingly, he thought we were closer to Calcutta than what we had calculated. He remembered passing through the town of Burdwan and did not think that it was too far from Panagarh. He told us that in his opinion they remained on the Grand Trunk (GT) Road all the way, and the cantonment area began on both sides of the road soon after the railway crossing. He had been taken to the Base Hospital which was quite a large establishment. According to Shah, Panagarh seemed to be a fairly large cantonment area. Although he was not certain but he thought that outside the camp boundary wall there was probably another electrified barbed wire fence.

Before I proceed further, let me provide a brief outline of the layout of the prison camp. If we were facing the road dividing the prisoner's camp from the guard's camp, there were two other similar twin sets of sheds adjacent and in sequence to our right. These were meant to house the Junior Commissioned officers (JCO) and Other Ranks (OR) respectively. As time went by these sheds began to fill up. The shed opposite to the officer's shed, comprised of camp officers, company kote, Medical Inspection (MI) Room, switch board for electric connections, and later on, the control of the PA equipment and loudspeakers. The living quarters of the unit guarding us were in various sheds opposite the JCO and OR compounds, the cook house being in the shed opposite to the one where the JCOs lived in. A barbed wire fence enclosed us within the parameters of the officer's compound which I shall henceforth refer to as the 'inner wire'. Each of the compounds was surrounded by its own inner wire. An outer wire enclosed the three compounds together and a wall serving as the fourth side of its perimeter. From the sound of traffic, particularly at night, we knew we were situated near a main road—I discovered later that it was, in fact, the GT Road. The surrounding wall was approximately 10 feet high. When we reached Panagarh, there was a high steel watchtower next to the wall between the JCO and OR compounds. In a short time thereafter four more wooden watchtowers were constructed at the four corners of the perimeter outside the outer wire. All watchtowers were manned by sentries during daytime and they would come down after dusk. A guard commander who was responsible for guarding the inner and outer gate patrolled the inner perimeter or stayed in a sentry box situated near us. The main gate of the prison camp was manned and the relief guard would rest next to the company kote.

Second Lt. Richard Scott, the junior-most of the three officers who were our 'keepers', in one of his chatty moods, informed us that the Panagarh Prison Camp had been sanctioned by the Indian Government to house the expected influx of Pakistani prisoners on or around 15 April 1971. A sum of Rs150,000 had been earmarked for this purpose. It seemed that the Indians were anticipating a substantial increase in our numbers and were certainly not sparing any expense in 'not interfering' in Pakistan's internal affairs. They expected this camp to eventually house up to a thousand prisoners. This did not happen until after the surrender in East Pakistan in 1971. When we walked into the POW's living shed on 30 April 1971, it contained 16 sets of beds, drawers, chairs and side tables. Our living area was not partitioned from the connecting shed which was to serve as an ante-cum-dining room. Everything was spick and span.

We soon had visitors. Brigadier Coelho, accompanied by Captain Chatterjee of the Rajput Regiment came the very first morning. He was all business and one could see that this camp was his particular 'baby'. Obviously he was someone who seemed serious about his responsibilities. He had given instructions that loudspeakers be obtained from the 'Signal Regiment' so that we were able to listen to news and songs. He warned us about the futility of 'monkey business' by informing us that even if we managed to escape from the camp, we will not be able to go too far since a decidedly hostile population was awaiting us outside. Brigadier Coelho told us that the entire world had turned against Pakistan, prophesizing with confidence that it was now only a matter of time before we ceased to exist. If our forefathers had paid heed to such 'prophets of doom', Pakistan would never have come into existence to begin with—hence we simply scoffed at him. We were nonplussed when he asked how many of us would like to go back to Pakistan, after which he stalked out sniggering with Chaterjee.

All guard duties were conducted by the book. The Standard Operating Procedure (SOP) to be followed was that whenever any Indian, irrespective of his rank, entered the compound, he was escorted by four sentries with fixed bayonets. Brigadiers and sweepers were rated the same escort. Pakistanis for them were dreaded creatures! Our continuous surveillance by sentries with bayonets did not faze us even for a moment. We became used to having loaded rifles pointed at us and went on with our business as usual.

Whenever a group of people are thrown together, they begin to look for familial ground. Sadiq Nawaz, Shah and I soon became quite friendly. Lt. Col. Khizar, Lt. Col. Aziz and Maj. Iqbal Ahmad formed a group of 'elders'. Capt. Ayaz and Lt. Amjad Saeed were with each other most of the time. Capt. Amin Ahmed Chaudhry mingled with everybody since he was confident that he would be leaving soon.

The EPR officers, Col. Aziz, Maj. Iqbal and Capt. Ayaz had managed to get away when a mutiny had broken out in their unit. They had initially succeeded in their escape but were ultimately surrounded in the Chittagong Hill Tracts. They were forced to surrender after a short fire-fight in which they exhausted their ammunition. They were lucky to have not been killed straightaway, and were subsequently handed over to Maj. Ziaur Rahman. He kept them in dignified captivity of sorts, before handing them over the Indians in the first week of April 1971. Both Col. Aziz and Maj. Iqbal were convinced that their families had been slaughtered by the roused population in the bloody orgy that followed their flight from Chittagong. As is natural under such conditions, this experience had affected them deeply. Col. Aziz, despondent and aloof, bore the stress and strain without exposing his actual feelings to us. Throughout the captivity he conducted himself in a dignified manner. The pain and anguish he must have been undergoing was hardly discernible in his demeanour and he remained a pillar of strength for his younger colleagues. Very correct in his attitude, he never made any attempts at over-riding the authority of Col. Khizar Hayat who was senior to him in rank. Most of the time he calmly played the role of an arbitrator between the younger officers with their firebrand ideas and the senior prisoners with their dogged, plodding ways, urging both to display restraint. Col. Aziz's admonishments were always meted with such affection that we did not feel bad, in fact, it would pacify us down.

Major Iqbal was very particular about carrying out his religious ritualistic duties. His nerves had become extremely taut due to his anxiety for his family's wellbeing which, understandably, can make a person difficult and cranky. As the days passed, he went into a state of acute depression that would oftentimes find an outlet in sudden outbursts. We at times feared that these outbursts might be symptomatic of an approaching mental breakdown. It would be unkind to blame him for his behaviour since he only had daughters who were in their teens— and it was but natural that he was fearful of their safety. He was never anxious for himself but only for his daughters.

Capt. Ayaz and Lt. Amjad were generally the most untroubled amongst us. What had happened and what was going to happen did not seem to faze them out. They were cracking jokes all the time. Although they were completely aware of the terrible calamity that had befallen their country in the form of a war, they were least concerned about what had taken place in East Pakistan. Their only concern was planning how to escape. As for me and Sadiq Nawaz, our arguments were mostly asinine since both of us would engage in debates adopting opposite stance that would invariably lead to fruitless arguments.

Major Sadiq Nawaz was a fine example of a patriot and a soldier and I would like to make special mention of him. He had all the ingredients of a fine human being. He was God fearing, kind, affectionate and sensitive. A man of conscience, his character was impeccable and he had the moral courage to voice his convictions. He had simple tastes, yet was sophisticated in his assessments. He was a fine example of an officer and a gentleman and a credit to the Pakistan Army.

As for myself, I am emotional and outspoken by nature, and often let my emotions get the better of me and also my behaviour. I am certain that these traits in me must have been unbearable for others at times but it is a characteristic that I have no control over.

NOTES

1. Deployed in great numbers in Panagarh during the Second World War, the United States' Air Force personnel included all sorts of support signals units and a major hospital complex. An American who was based in Panagarh at that time records in his *Octogenarian Diary* that the outfit 'was stationed outside a village named Panagarh in the province of Bihar, an impoverished region about 100 miles northwest of Calcutta.' One of the primary outfits then assigned to Panagarh was the 1st Air Commandos. Its main mission was to fly gliders carrying Special Force units who were dropped behind Japanese lines in neighbouring Burma.

   A significant figure related to Panagarh was UK's famed Brigadier Orde Wingate who had been posted as Commander of the famous 'Chindits', a mixed Indian and British force that specialized in guerrilla warfare. A controversial figure, Wingate had been posted out from Palestine because of his pro Zionist leanings and his moves to counter the Arab action against Jewish settlers. He also made efforts to raise a Jewish force. Wingate was killed in late 1944 when his glider crashed in the Burmese jungles. The ferry aircraft was believed to have taken off from Panagarh.

   One amazing coincidence was that in August 1947 Panagarh became an assembly point for units earmarked for Pakistan. Two 'Musalmaan' companies moved by train under command of my father Capt. (later Lt. Col.) Abdul Majeed Sehgal from Panagarh to Lahore [and onto Sialkot].

2. The sacrifice of the Delta Company 27 Baluch is one of the great tragedies of the Pakistan Army. By some coincidence one of my living heroes Major (later Lt. Gen.) Leharasab Khan was posted to the 27 Baluch in 1971. The 1E Bengal where he had been commissioned had revolted in Jessore. Leharasab Khan was badly wounded near Khulna in November 1971 and left for dead. My platoon commander at the PMA, Lt. Col. (later Lt. Gen.) Imtiazullah Warraich who was commanding a unit of the Punjab Regiment that was withdrawing was passing by in his jeep. He spotted Leharasab Khan and brought him to the Jessore Airfield which was next to the Combined Military Hospital. He was lucky to be immediately evacuated by the last helicopter to Dacca, and then was again lucky that he was one of the seriously wounded to be evacuated by the last aircraft to leave Dacca for Karachi.

5

DEVIL'S ADVOCATE

Till now the interrogations conducted by the Indians had been quite straightforward, although, the ability of the interrogators[1] varied. The army teams were certainly better than the Border Security Force (BSF) which is more used to using coercive and third degree methods. We had so far not encountered anyone who was impressive enough except for Colonel Menon who was most certainly from the army deployed in Agartala. We became used to basic forms of interrogation applied to us and hence were not prepared for what was soon about to befall on us. For the benefit of those who are not familiar with interrogations one must at least give them a whiff of what was in store for the POWs. Resort to brutal, third degree methods do result in the extraction of information, but the tormented is most likely to confess to what the tormentors are wanting to hear. It may *not* be the truth that the torturers are looking for.

The technique of interrogation that we were subjected to in Panagarh was sophisticated. They used the technique of profiling our personality and then using it against us. This was a dangerous development and since none of us had ever been aware of such a technique, we were falling into the trap of our interrogator, with unfortunate consequences.

Although we generally knew about the RAW, none of us possessed much information about it. Our general impression was that RAW was very similar to the Central Intelligence Agency (CIA) and the Inter-Services Intelligence (ISI). In terms of achievement, it seems that RAW has proven to be very successful.

The month of April passed without any change. It was in May that Malhotra walked into our lives. I single Malhotra out because his method of interrogation was unique, and so were his goals. By the time he left Panagarh, he had managed to sow the seeds of deep dissension among us. He succeeded because he was clever; we failed because of our simplicity and hence fell into his web of intrigues and deception. The experience that we had with him must be recorded as a lesson for future soldiers to come. His spectre haunted the camp and such an atmosphere was created by him that it continued even after he was long gone.

The moment we saw Malhotra, tall, slim and bespectacled, get out of the jeep with the Camp Commandant riding in the back, we could guess that this was a man of some importance, even though he was in civilian clothes. After some time he accompanied Major Uppal to the shed. The Camp Commandant seemed to have a change of heart overnight and was unduly concerned about us. He enquired us about our welfare. Within the first few sentences that were articulated by Malhotra, we could gather that he was a 'headshrinker' of sorts—there was no doubt about it. He also seemed to have plenty of clout. While we could logically guess that he wanted information out of us, we could not make out his actual task. We were on unfamiliar territory—soldiers rarely experience an encounter with psychiatrists and psychologists. We were quite unprepared for what we were about to face and gawked at him in awe. Malhotra later commented humorously on our bemused expressions when we had initially seen him—and that we gaped at him as if he was a monster of sorts. The same day he called for the junior-most among us, Ataullah Shah, and conversed with him for almost two hours. This was strange! In the meantime there was much banging and thumping as a new compartment was being put together with tin sheets in the opposite shed. We braced ourselves for the worst. When Shah came back, we bombarded him with questions. What we could glean from his answers confirmed our worst suspicions—that the objective of Malhotra was to attempt at brainwashing us. For us Pakistanis the word 'brainwashing' arouses memories of the sophisticated tactics of brain-washing that were used by advanced countries for the pursuance of their objectives. According to Shah, he had been subjected to a preliminary. We reserved the exercise of our full mental processes till we got fuller information about the tactics of our enemy [Malhotra] on this new battleground. Visions of Gary Powers, the U-2 Pilot who took off from an airbase near Peshawar in 1960 and was shot down by the Soviets over Russia flitted through us.

More civilians were seen coming to the camp bearing briefcases and suspicious looking gadgets, probably cameras and tape-recorders. Obviously they were part of Malhotra's team. The new cubicle in the shed that was being built had been completed. From then henceforth it came to be known as the 'Headshrinkers Room'. We gathered our nerves to face Malhotra. When Malhotra came the next morning, he told us that he had been informed that we had misgivings about his arrival. He assured us that he had simply come to ease the tension and pressures that we were undergoing. Some consolation indeed!

We found Malhotra to be quite affable. He distributed cigarettes among the three smokers: Lt. Col. Aziz Sheikh, Major Sadiq and Ataullah Shah. He was not happy with the quality of the cigarettes that were being issued to us and assured us that he would ensure better quality in the future—which never did happen. He was polite to all of us and his manner was appropriately differential to the senior ones amongst us. All in all he succeeded in creating a favourable impression which we conceded to, albeit grudgingly.

Next day, around 9 am Shah was again called into the 'Headshrinker's Room'. There was no sign of him or Malhotra even after lunch hours. At 6 pm the gates of our sheds were shut as usual. Shortly after, through our peepholes we saw Shah and Malhotra emerge smoking cigarettes. Shah did not seem particularly disturbed which was encouraging. It seemed that the youngest of our lot had withstood the 'brainwashing' quite well! Seeing Shah looking cheerful was encouraging. At 11 pm Shah finally returned to the shed. He was suffering from a splitting headache and could barely stand. Fussing over him, we helped him get into bed. From what we could gather from his fragmented speech was that around 5 pm he had been given an injection after which he does not remember what happened. This was news to us! When we had seen him come out with Malhotra at 6 pm, they were chatting and smoking away. Shah told us that Malhotra asked him questions regarding me and Sadiq. Shah was worried for us. Although we tried to make light of it, we did feel troubled at Malhotra's interest in us. While we massaged Shah's head, Sadiq and I glanced at each other with growing stirrings of dread. For us brainwashing meant that if we did not cooperate, we would be turned into living vegetables which was worse than death—it was living death. Overnight the menace of Malhotra began to assume gigantic proportions. However, Pakistani youth does not indulge in pessimism for long. Sadiq, Ayaz, Amjad and I amused ourselves by imitating the listless, mindless beings we would become once Malhotra was done with us. Morbid humour can be a pleasant distraction.

In between invoking the blessings of God on Shah, Col. Khizar asked him if Malhotra allowed prisoners to go to the bathroom! The Colonel had a way of mixing humour with sobriety, hence, one was not certain whether to laugh with him or at him. Col. Khizar's turn was due the next morning and we got up early to regale him with good natured banter as to what all Malhotra would do to him. We jested with him that since he possessed more experience, Malhotra must be itching to get his unholy hands on him. The Colonel bore our banter with silence and when Malhotra came the next day, he went along with him like a docile lamb being taken for slaughter. By this time we had nicknamed Malhotra 'Leary' (after Doctor Timothy Leary, the high priest of LSD, a psychoactive hallucinogenic drug).

Lt. Col. Aziz Sheikh advised us that the best way to deal with Malhotra was not to allow ourselves to be entrapped into any kind of discussion on any subject. Although this was sensible advice, it was easier said than done. Moreover, as a youngster, one tends to get into fiery debates and heated arguments in defence of one's country. Colonel Khizar was back after a few hours, and Colonel Aziz was back in even less time. Major Iqbal who was by now suffering from acute depression was away much longer. He told us that Malhotra, upon noticing that he was mentally agitated, spent a lot of time talking to him. Malhotra even assured Major Iqbal that he would try and find out the whereabouts of his family. Hence Major Iqbal returned looking quite appeased. None of the subsequent officers who were questioned mentioned any sort of medication being injected into them. Major Iqbal went successively for three days and for two hours. After each session he seemed in better spirits. Malhotra had instructed all of us to write letters to our families which would be posted home. Since desperate men will clutch onto the last straw, we gradually began to acquire more trust in Malhotra, in spite of our reservations.

My rendezvous with the 'Headshrinker' across the table materialized at about 9 am on 25 May 1971. Since Malhotra's arrival, the conditions inside the POW Camp, which the Indians persisted in calling a Detention Camp, had improved. Newspapers and magazines seemed to mushroom around the place. For the first time we were able to read foreign magazines such the *Time* and *Newsweek*. These magazines were full of tales of atrocities unleashed by the Pakistan Army in East Pakistan, hence, the Indians happily allowed us to read them. The loudspeaker blared out daily news and innumerable songs, morning and evening. For a day or so, the shed door was kept open beyond the normal closing time so that we could sit outside till after dusk. A relaxed atmosphere seemed to pervade all around us. During this time, we reached the climax of the good treatment ever accorded to us by the Indians. Therefore when I sat face to face with Malhotra, I was not adversely disposed towards him, though I remained on my guard because I could understand that it was this man's intention to make me commit something, even inadvertently, which would be detrimental to my interests and to that of my country. He had a very condescending manner about him and spoke in very precise English. After what I had already heard about him from others, I could not but admire his capabilities. Even the devil must get his due! I was also curious to know what made him tick.

After the exchange of normal niceties between us, he then began with the business of the day, remarking that since time immemorial India had tried to be a friendly neighbour to Pakistan. That qualifies as the single most untrue statement made in one breath that I had ever heard in my life. Switching from one topic to another, pinning you on certain facts, discussing seemingly irrelevant subjects such as cricket for a long period and then suddenly producing books and pamphlets to impress upon you his knowledge of Pakistan Army's formations, units, arms and equipment, he would go on to discuss some out of the way subject, shift onto international relations and then spend some time to see whether you were ready to loosen up on military subjects.

All of us remained on our guard regarding what we divulged since we knew that our conversations were being tape-recorded—one inadvertent slip from us and we would have fallen into his game plan. He attempted to convince me that all that had taken place was Zulfikar Ali Bhutto's fault and if he carried on in this way it would mean the destruction of Pakistan. I told him that if this was the case, the Indians should be happy with Bhutto since the Indians had the aim of destroying Pakistan. Conversely, I told him, that since the Indians thought this of Bhutto, the opposite was probably truer. We ran into blank walls as far as Bhutto was concerned. He then switched onto a different line of argument in pursuing the same topic. He asked me as to who were responsible for the present crisis. I said to him that while the Awami League had clearly won the elections, the concentration of their votes and seats thereof showed that their mandate extended only within East Pakistan. Hence, they would have to go into a coalition with other political parties from West Pakistan in order to form a government and run the country.

Malhotra did not try to inject me with anything. I had carried a nail hidden with me in case he attempted anything. He told me a little about himself and asked me whether I wanted to broadcast any message to my family, which I declined with a polite thank you and said that our letters to our families should be enough to reassure them. At one stage he asked me what all did we talk about. I told him that he should know since he had the shed 'bugged'. He did not raise the subject again though he did try it on a different tack, by writing short notes on everyone and inviting comments. I withheld from commenting. Malhotra did bring a chocolate cake on 31 May 71 and tried to pull that to his advantage. In was a moment of Sadiq's weakness. He took him to the Officer's Mess for tea and repeatedly asked him to broadcast a message to his family. I am proud of Major Sadiq Nawaz because I remember his anguish that day, but he was a soldier and an officer and flatly refused the temptation offered to him. Malhotra remained without a pigeon. Sadiq, Amjad and Ayaz went through the same kind of grilling as I did with Malhotra on successive days. He then moved on to other ranks. We would brief them as best as we could on what they should expect during interrogation. Shah was to serve as interpreter during the interrogation of the Pathan Other Ranks (OR).

At this point Amjad and Ayaz insinuated that Shah was probably playing the Indian game. I laughed this off as conjecture on their part because Shah, being the youngest, had become quite a favourite with us. Moreover, it did not seem strange to us that Shah being Pustho speaking should go along as an interpreter. What did not cross our minds was that the OR's spoke Urdu fluently! It seems the Pathan POWs were subjected to a concentrated dose of Khan Abdul Ghaffar Khan and the Pakhtoonistan issue. We were informed by Shah that the OR's were brilliant at evading Malhotra's questions.

It is all very well for me to recount all this but the fact of the matter is that none of us should have entered into a conversation with Malhotra. For POWs, the only answer is to give your name, rank and serial number. However this is easier said than done. Obviously no army wants its soldiers to become POWs and that is why 'how to face your interrogators in case you become a POW' is never taught as a subject. Some via media must be found to ensure that soldiers do not fall prey to predators of the mind like Malhotra. We were not fooling him at any time. To put it bluntly, we were making bloody fools out of ourselves by engaging with him. I was at fault and I make no excuses.

We did not realize it at the time but in the carefree atmosphere that Malhotra had created, he had also instilled an undercurrent of suspicion. I have reason to believe now that it may have been a figment of imagination and circumstances. We had become wary of each other, something we were not previously. It was not so visible then but when circumstances changed and tempers began to fray, suspicion reared its ugly head and threatened to destroy the façade of unity amongst us. We were all at blame, however, luckily no lasting damage was achieved.

Malhotra had clearly come for a purpose. But he derived negligible information from us. Neither did he make much of an effort to 'brainwash' us. In fact he was insisting that we should communicate with our families through radio broadcasts. So what was the purpose of his visit to the camp? Why had he spent so much time discussing matters of insignificance?

Looking back now, it seems clear to me as to the reason of his troubles. He was assessing each one of us.

Malhotra had come to see if he could bargain for our souls.

Thus he was playing the role of the 'Devil's Advocate'!

NOTE

1. According to the US Army Technical Manual: 'an important aspect of interrogation is how you make the "approach".' Successful questioning of a POW may never materialize without proper contact and the situation is likely to get out of control and degenerate into an argument. The decision as to what approach to employ depends both on the interrogator's psychological evaluation of the POW and on the personality of the interrogator. Interrogators conscientiously strive to increase their knowledge of human behaviour and practical psychology to be able to accomplish their mission. The US Army Manual further states that, 'Applied Psychology' is merely the application of such tendencies mentioned to interrogation techniques.

   However interrogation techniques are more or less similar everywhere. The interrogator applies his knowledge of human behaviour by purposely avoiding certain questions during interrogation and substituting other questions, or by assuming certain moods or attitudes because he thinks that it will bear more productive results. At the outset the objective of an interrogation is seldom to obtain an admission or a confession. The subject is interrogated for accurate and reliable information. The use of physical or psychological duress in this type of situation is generally unproductive and an indication of frustration and lack of ability on the part of the interrogator. The approaches are limited to the initiative, imagination, and ingenuity of the interrogator; can be tailored to suit each individual case, and may be combined with other methods to suit special requirements. The methods used may be: (1) Direct approach; (2) Stressing the futility of withholding information since defeat is already inevitable for the subject's country, force, or unit. Further, that the information no longer has any significance, since the situation under discussion has already culminated and their fellow POWs have already given all the relevant information; (3) Rapid fire questioning method where the POW is constantly on the defensive and off balance thereby weakening resistance and/or his determination to give evasive answers; (4) Emotional approach, i.e., playing upon the emotions of the POW to obtain information; (5) Use of trickery which has limitless variations, its purpose being to cause the POW to divulge information without him being actually aware of it. The methods used are: sympathy, sternness, pride, bluff, fear, threat-and-rescue approach.

Another important aspect that needs mention is the use of drugs on prisoners. The so-called 'silent drug', a pharmacologically potent substance given to a person unaware of its administration, can make possible the induction of a hypnotic trance in a previously unwilling subject. Particularly important is matching the drug to the personality of the prisoner. Their function is to cause capitulation and shift from resistance to cooperation. Once this shift has been accomplished, coercive techniques can be abandoned both for moral reasons and because they are unnecessary and even counter-productive. But certain drugs 'may give rise to psychotic manifestations such as hallucinations, delusions or disorientation', so that 'the verbal material obtained cannot always be considered valid.'

6

UPPAL'S IRE

Time and tide waits for no man . . . and yet time is endless. When time hangs heavy on one's hands it turns into agony. Boredom sets in—and along with it an idle mind—the devil's workshop. The month of June, true to form, was sultry and hot. To round off an ill-starred week we had our inevitable brush with two Indian Non-Commissioned Officers (NCO) we labelled as the 'Unholy Twins'. The material effects of our brush with authority was that we had no newspapers, books, magazines, chess or cards to keep us entertained in our moments of boredom, and also no Malhotra[1] to salvage our creature comforts for us.

We resorted to innovations to reduce the boredom and listlessness which was dulling our senses. The only resort left to us was either to while away our time gazing at the sentries or bicker endlessly with each other. The few songs that were played again and again over the PA system had begun to irritate us. We were becoming edgy—it is funny how people begin to get on each others nerves when thrown together under such trying circumstances. Trivial issues become a matter of grave importance—to be argued and quarrelled over.

I was also inflicted by the damages of such circumstances. In retrospect, I am sorry to have placed myself in a situation where Scott and the Unholy Twins were allowed to get the better of me over an insignificant matter and which resulted in the loss of our privileges. Although, my fellow inmates tried to make me feel better by assuring me that they did not care about the privileges, I nonetheless felt guilty on that score. Although we remained united in our common front against the enemy, we were beginning to get polarized into separate groups. This was not a desirable development—in fact it was detrimental for all of us. Yet people become weak when faced with a situation like ours. Our emotions were getting the better of our reasoning—we were becoming unbearable for each other.

In our motley group, Sadiq Nawaz and I qualified as being more emotional in nature. We had a full-blown argument over such a trivial matter that in the end we did not even remember what the argument was all about. In a matter of moments undeserving accusations were flying back and forth, and before we knew it we were at each other's throats. But the argument subsided as suddenly as it had flared up. We were embracing each other after a day, and I admitted that it was more my fault than his. Ayaz and Amjad were happy at our conciliation. We were partners in a greater venture and it did not behove us to engage in petty squabbles amongst ourselves. However one surprising element emerged out of this incident. It was the unexpected behaviour from Shah on whom we had all been showering our affections. He began to quietly build up a common front of senior officers against us, particularly against me. For lack of any logical explanation for this, I can only guess that it was due to my views on escape plans. And hence for the short period that Sadiq had been estranged from us, Shah had a field-day. Ayaz, Amjad and I were considerably taken aback. There was no conceivable reason for this display of Shah's animosity. As soon as Sadiq patched up with me, the senior officers, under the clear urgings of Shah, stopped talking to Sadiq and me. The resultant boycott ended our supply of cigarettes of which Shah was the source who would wangle them out of the sentries. Sadiq being a smoker suffered the most. Only a smoker can truly know the suffering that he undergoes when a cigarette is denied to him. But Sadiq also remained steadfast in his stance of not asking the smoking clique, who were acting up, for a cigarette. Ayaz, Amjad and I launched a 'cigarette' campaign. This was perhaps a wrong move on our part because it became symbolic of our dissent and only widened the gap between us. The immediate outcome was the exchange of hot words between Sadiq and Lt. Col. Aziz across the table over another trivial matter. If Col. Aziz who had a cool and calm persona could lose his temper, then matters were too far-gone indeed. Shah in the meantime could be seen dancing full attention on the beck-and-call of the three senior officers.

At this stage Capt. Chatterjee, an officer of Bengali origin belonging to the Rajput Regiment, made one of his periodic visits to the camp. Tall, slim, fair, and smartly dressed, Chatterjee was an interesting character. One could even deem him as handsome but in a slimy sort of way. Two rows of ribbons were dressed upon his chest. He had a tendency to swagger rather than walk. He was probably either Staff Captain or Station Staff Officer or some such exalted position—in any case he let it be known to us that he was responsible for the local administration of the camp. He would barge into the camp gunning an

MP's jeep in a manner which signified to the whole world in general, and us prisoners in particular, his utter disdain and contempt for anything which did not entirely meet his standards, the lofty heights of which we could never fully comprehend. The poor MP's jeep was driven with complete disregard. The Camp Commandant was either in awe of him as is usual in such circumstances since he was the Staff Officer, or he was a good friend of his, because even though Uppal was a Major, it was always Chatterjee who was the Master of Ceremonies during their round of our shed. Chatterjee's conversations with us were usually a one-sided monologue of sneers and sarcasm. In the manner of all Babus attempting to be Sahibs, he would try to speak precise, modulated English, but his Bengali accent was too pronounced and would give him away: someone trying to pretend what he wasn't. In comparison to Chatterjee, Uppal seemed like an angel.

Into our faction-ridden midst, Chatterjee strode in one day, clutching a newspaper. He thought it befitting to first inform Lt. Col. Khizar Hayat what he thought of us for misbehaving with Scott. In an over-bearing tone he defined the singular elements of our 'atrocious behaviour'—our conduct was despicable. He then told us that we were not doing any favours by being in the camp, and also that we were on no picnic. He gave us the distinct impression that, in fact, it was he who was favouring us by keeping us at the camp. Finally, in precise tones, he gave us a lecture on the fundamentals of good behaviour. When Chatterjee became too excited he would flounder in his exposition of the English language and I would get really worried that he might exhaust his vocabulary. He once waved a newspaper in front of us asking us to read what Anthony Mascarenhas had written about the 'genocide' in East Pakistan. He had highlighted the portions that illustrated the murders, arson and rape perpetrated by the Bengali elements in Chittagong. I considered this act of Chatterjee's as one of the most despicable acts of sadism that I have come across in my life. Although crude and insensitive, yet this episode bore significant results. Lt. Col. Aziz Sheikh's and Maj. Iqbal's immediate families were located in Chittagong—they had received no news of them and were worried sick for their safety. They were constantly thinking about their children. I too had a few near and dear ones living in Chittagong and was naturally worried about them. Therefore Chatterjee's brandishing the article at us was cruelty par excellence. Our tears of sorrow turned into tears of frustration and anger. They drew us together in a manner that we should have remained in the first instance. In this sense, one should be grateful to Chatterjee. He undid what Malhotra had succeeded in doing, i.e., create a rift among us.

Shah did something most generous. He came up to me and embraced me declaring that we were brothers. Such gestures are not easily forgotten. The emotional outburst against Chatterjee had forged us together once more. Almost simultaneously we were once again allowed our 'privileges'. The sun was shining again. The reaction to the spill-over of our emotions was that we began to discern freedom in the air. Col. Khizar was confident that the Indians would release us soon. Since we Pakistanis are incurable optimists, we took note of all portents and interpreted them to mean that we were going home soon. When will we ever learn?

The senior JCO of 430 Field Company, a talkative soul named Paniacker, told Col. Khizar in confidence that we would be taken on a tour of India before we were sent back to Pakistan. Malhotra had also informed us on more or less the same lines—that we would be shown some places of interest in India. Putting our amateur detective prowess at work, we anticipated that our day of release was very close. The atmosphere of the camp had also lightened considerably. Scott came and inquired from us whether on Sunday we would like Madrasi food for breakfast. There was a flood of newspapers and magazines, and fresh soaps and toothpastes were sanctioned to us. Freedom was in the air!

In addition to being optimists we Pakistanis are also great cynics that sums up the complete portrait of our contradictory nature. We love to deride ourselves about the arrival of good fortune as being too good to be true. Hence, Sadiq, Ayaz, Amjad and I scoffed at such news, proclaiming that this was probably a gimmick by the JCO in order to make us behave ourselves for the time being. However, in our hearts, we hoped that this was not the case and that we were in fact close to freedom. Havaldar Clerk Dubarry who would, at opportune moments, sometimes chat with us across the wire told us categorically that an exchange of prisoners was going to take place in accordance with the Geneva Convention. A mood of anticipation set in. Hence the month of June ended with all of us in an upbeat mood.

Uppal who had conveniently sprained his ankle soon after his wife came back from home, had disappeared from the scene for a couple of days. As soon as he came back, he came around and seemed genuinely concerned about our welfare. Around the beginning of July, the camp underwent a process of thorough cleaning and sprucing up. It became apparent that a visitor was due. Our latrine, which had been flooded due to the incessant rains, was being replaced with a new latrine made of bricks. Opinions as to who the visitors were varied. Some of us thought that the visitors were possibly either officials of the Red Cross, or they could also be the British MPs who had been visiting India during that time. Some were of the view that it was the Swiss Ambassador and that we would be repatriated along with the Pakistan Deputy High Commission personnel who were virtually interned in Calcutta. Paniacker took the cake—he thought that we would be visited by the Viceroy's daughter. We gathered that he meant the British Peeress who was also in India at the time. We were agog at this prospect and got busy in sprucing ourselves up. It had been a long time since we had seen a woman.

The great day came. An MP's jeep arrived first—four MPs were sitting in full ceremonial regalia. It was followed by a black car. Whoever they might be, it was definitely no female. A man alighted from the car to a flurry of salutes. Our first reaction was that of disappointment. Firstly, the man didn't look British and secondly, he was certainly no lady. Our visitor was in civilian clothes and was accompanied by another man also wearing civilian attire. He acknowledged the salutes in a 'civilian fashion'. The VIP was short, stocky and fair and had a glass eye. He spoke in Urdu in a sing-song manner. His companion was tall, fair, with a slightly reddish tone, and brown hair. They took a tour of the camp with the VIP displaying genuine interest. He went around enquiring about our welfare and whether we had any complaints, in a manner of a hotel manager of a five-star hotel querying the hotel guests. Lt. Col. Khizar Hayat spoke on behalf of all of us and requested him that our government be informed about us, and furthermore, that we should be granted permission to write and receive letters. The VIP instructed his companion to note down all our demands and told us that he would 'pose' our issues with the proper authorities. He then bid his farewell with the same fanfare as his arrival.

As regards his identity we were stumped. Col. Khizar maintained that the VIP's companion was Russian and no amount of good natured derision at this astounding assessment would make him change his mind. However Paniacker, in one of his ramblings, let it slip that the VIP was an Adjutant General, and that they had served together in the 2nd Airborne Division in Malir Cantonment in Pakistan during World War II and afterwards also. This confirmed our views that he was either GOC, Bengal Area, or he was maybe Adjutant General of the Indian

Army, and whose identity the Indians wanted to maintain a state secret. Some countries believe in keeping everything clandestine.

Immediately after the visit, Shah was instructed to pack his stuff for a move to another undisclosed destination. He was to be taken there along with some Pathan JCOs and ORs. From the sentries we wheedled out that they were bound for Calcutta. Since it was an all Pathan contingent, hence, we thought that they would probably be freed on the 'Pakhtoonistan' card. Whatever it may be, for us it meant that one of us was being freed—which also meant that someone would be carrying news about us back home. With emotions of both envy and joy, we looked on as Shah left us clutching his meagre possessions with him. At that moment we all wished that all of us had been Pashto-speaking!

One night, after about three days, Shah was back along with the others. Though disappointed that he had not been set free as we had surmised, we were nevertheless delighted to see him, if only to glean some news about how the outside world looked like. It seems that the Indians had tried a dash of the 'Pakhtoonistan' stunt. According to Shah, they were also subjected to some interrogation. He narrated his adventure in some detail. We were more interested in the route and conditions outside the camp. Hence we cross-examined Shah till he was probably completely exasperated with us. Of material interest to us was the fact that he had brought another towel and some toothpaste. We really cursed him for not smuggling in the civilian clothes that were handed out to him in Calcutta.

A day or so later a statement supposed to have been made by Shah was published in the newspapers. It possessed an anti-Pakistan tone to it. We were quite taken aback at this and naturally questioned Shah. Looking back on it now, I feel that Shah deserved an Oscar award for having fooled us into thinking that he was completely oblivious of what was happening. We told him to protest this outrage, which he said he had done in an interview with Major Uppal. However, suspicion and mistrust had again reared its ugly head over the camp. Naib Subedar Aurangzeb, who had been admitted to CMH Barrackpore with a broken ankle, also came back in the same truck. When we met him, we asked him for some money. He told us to ask Shah since he had been kept in a hotel in Calcutta. He also told us that Shah had spoken on the radio but at the time we thought that this was an exaggeration and that the JCO was probably prejudiced. However we became wary of Shah—and understandably so, although, we sincerely hoped that all our doubts were baseless.

It was around the tenth of July that we learned that it was now Amin's turn for the wild blue yonder. Since Amin was segregated from us, we would only occasionally get to talk to him. Before he went away, he came to bid us goodbye. It was more or less certain that Amin was going back to join the newly formed 'Mukti Bahini' or 'Freedom Brothers' as the new Bangladesh Army was being called. For old time's sake, we requested him to inform our families in Pakistan of our welfare. Since he did not know anyone in any foreign country and he could not possibly correspond directly to anyone in Pakistan, I gave him the address of someone I knew in Hong Kong through whom he could establish contact with Pakistan. Unfortunately, Scott who had been watching us like a hawk body-searched Amin as soon as he returned to his shed, found and snatched away the piece of paper on which I had written the address. This was exactly what Scott had been out to achieve—to throw bait at his arch enemy—which was me, and then bring him down to a position of complete compromise. He literally flounced off to Major Uppal to report my misdeeds to him. He was in his elements. I went through a very painful interview with Maj. Uppal the same evening. The gist of Uppal's anger was that he would certainly deal with me as he had been planning to do for some time. He said that he would make sure that when I went out of the camp it would be on my knees.

Next morning, after Amin had been taken away, I was moved to the shed where he had been kept. I was to be kept in solitary confinement and my 'privileges' were forfeited. I was not to move out of the shed except on extreme calls of nature and not talk to anybody. Part of the furniture was taken away from me. I was not to have the benefit of the fans, recently installed, at anytime, night or day. Moreover, I was put on half rations as is the norm in solitary confinement. When I requested that my supply of cigarettes, tea and fruits not be stopped—they were stopped immediately. Fortunately, they did not know that I did not smoke and seldom drank tea or ate fruits—so it did not bother me. All these measures were to be enforced with immediate effect.

Every one should undergo the experience of a solitary confinement. The lone sojourn only serves to resolve all doubts prevailing in one's mind. I went into solitary confinement with a singularly deadly purpose—I wanted to be out of this damned place. As far as I was concerned this was a blessing in disguise and I meant to take full advantage of the situation. But being kept in isolation has its advantages and disadvantages. The one thing that I missed was that I could not get

to talk to my comrades except in the bathroom, and that too whenever
we could manage it. Even Shah rose to the occasion, and twice managed
to smuggle in newspapers for me to read. Words of encouragement
floated to me from my comrades—all this served to keep me quite
pepped up. I had made up my mind to escape and Sadiq gave me the
go-ahead in attempting an exit from the shed. My actual escape attempt
was left by tacit understanding to his approval for later.

Subramaniam had been replaced by another Quartermaster Havaldar
in June, whose name I never got to know. This was a most beneficial
change. He was simply wonderful. Despite the Commandant's orders, I
was given my full scale of rations, in fact, more than that. Some Indian
soldiers would cheer me up with words of encouragement to ward off
my loneliness. This particular Quartermaster Havaldar was a good
human being, and even though he was an enemy, I have no hesitation
in declaring that he was one of the few genuine soldiers that I came
across in India.

I received a visit from Chatterjee the Rajput. He at first feigned
surprise at seeing me there and then said it was all part of the game. He
said that since I had done something—in consequence they would do
something. He made it clear to me that I was justified in what I had
done and that as a result of that, the Indians were justified in clamping
their punishment upon me. He was very cocksure and had a tut-tut
attitude about him. In a burst of generosity he told me that I could have
anything I wanted (such as books etc.) if I bore my punishment without
any trouble. At this I became a little worked up with him and told him
where exactly he could dump his generosity. There was quite a scene.
Probably diagnosing me as a madcap, the Rajput made a hasty retreat.
I could see that he was ruffled and felt satisfied. Such episodes were
interesting pastimes that kept me occupied.

Scott was in his elements. I could see him strutting about, increasing
restrictions upon me. Even the sentries began to display signs of
exasperation. He spoke to my comrades in a boisterous manner only to
enhance my sense of loneliness. In a perverse sort of way I aught to be
grateful to Scott—by torturing me and making my life unbearable, he
made my resolve to escape even stronger. I had been converted into a
desperado. My mind was now perfectly geared for an escape attempt!

The die had been cast!

It was now or never!

NOTE

1. From my conversations with Malhotra I gathered that the Indians were particularly allergic to Zulfikar Ali Bhutto. Also, China was one of Malhotra's nightmares. The Indians were of the impression that Chinese were lurking everywhere in Pakistan; Chinese troops were overflowing at the Pak/China border; Chinese gunboats were all over the coast of both East and West Pakistan.

On the Kashmir issue, Malhotra maintained that we Pakistanis had been the aggressors all along. Regarding the Indian interference in East Pakistan, Malhotra's contention was that the Indians had done nothing to aggravate the crisis, in fact, they were the sufferers because they had to deal with a large influx of refugees. I told him that with all the arms and ammunition now loose in Indian Eastern states, India had in fact dug its own grave and the refugee problem which it had trumpeted so much about would aggravate their law and order problems.

Malhotra began to talk about himself. His family belonged to Sindh and he had retired from the Indian Army as a Major. When I asked him what he did for a living he said that he worked for the 'Psychological Wing'.

7

SADIQ NAWAZ EXPRESS

Nobody plans to fail—people fail to plan.

A plan of escape has to be worked out before one can begin to dream of freedom. It is very easy to elude ourselves after the danger is over that we went about our dilemma in a cold, rational and logical manner—in our case nothing can be further from the truth. We were dedicated to a purpose and yet we lacked that singular act of concerted direction that is imperative for producing an effective plan of operations. In the Military Academy our instructors would insist on 'purpose' and 'determination'. It is inculcated in us that to overcome a dangerous situation it is vital to carry on with determination and purpose.

In the evaluation of the plan, coherent bits of information were accumulated and were subsequently used by me in my escape bid. My escape was a team effort of Sadiq, Ayaz, Amjad and myself. It was with their blessings that I availed the first available chance. It was with Sadiq's guidance that we acquired all the facts and incorporated it in the escape plan. There was no doubt that Sadiq Nawaz was my guide and mentor. Having been commissioned into the Engineer Corps, Sadiq opted for the Special Services Group (SSG). After a longish stint in the SSG he was transferred from Engineers to Infantry, being posted to 4E Bengal at Comilla. As a trained commando officer, such kinds of operations were a part of his existence. He had to provide the executive cover that was needed to even indulge in such liberal thoughts as to the acquisition of freedom on our own initiative. Hence it can be said that he was the brains and the spirit behind my escape. Although Ayaz had done the SSG course, he was not inducted into the commandos. I had only completed the ad-hoc course conducted by Brig. A.O. Mehta in Comilla in early 1966, after the war with India in 1965.

We had read about numerous wartime escape episodes. I had also seen a number of movies made on the subject that included: *The Great Escape, The One That Got Away,* and *Von Ryan's Express.* But there is no set model to follow—the conditions vary according to the circumstances.

However the principles remain the same. Escape, evasion and survival is also taught as a subject in military schools. I was lucky that I had done a short course under [then] Major Nusratullah,[1] an acknowledged specialist, having been one of the first to be part of the fledging Special Services Group (SSG) raised as 19 Baluch in Chirat, and trained by US Special Forces and CIA teams.

We collected and collated whatever guidelines that we could think of. Having gone through our requirements and conditions, the most fitting word that could describe our escape was 'impossible'. However 'impossible' is one word of the English language, the meaning of which is largely lost on hereditary optimists fired by enthusiasm. It is also said that it simply takes longer to do the impossible. It did occur to me that having enjoyed movies on wartime escape in the comparative comfort of freedom—in actuality it is much more difficult than what is portrayed. There is a likelihood that as the days go by, positivism begins to get overshadowed by cynicism and pessimism. Inconsequential matters assume gigantic proportions. Hence it is imperative to work towards freedom very fast.

One may take any number of courses and spend as many number of hours of training, but when the situation becomes alive—one is an amateur at the business. We naturally jumbled up all our priorities—it took us a while to start thinking like professionals. We naturally could not afford to put down all our plans on paper because of the surprise inspections. Our assessments and evaluations therefore remained vague and abstract for the most part.

A plan of escape has to be broken into various phases and the necessities of each phase worked out:

- Phase One   — Break out from camp
- Phase Two   — Ex-filtration from camp
- Phase Three — Maximum distance from camp
- Phase Four   — Ex-filtration from India

The first two phases naturally received our fullest attention; the details and the means for accomplishing them fully rested on our own ingenuity. The next phases depended by and large on our physical fitness. There was a dearth of possibilities for the fourth phase and no definite solution. This phase required combining all of our physical and mental resources together. Also, we needed to work backwards from Phase Two in order to successfully launch Phase One. These two phases primarily depended on the best available moment for us in the camp, an opportunity that must be taken or missed forever. Phases Three and Four depended to a great extent on the atmosphere prevailing inside India at that time. The salient bits of information that in our minds were absolutely necessary before we initiated our escape plan were:

- Layout of the camp
- Habits of the sentries and the guard commanders
- Means of exit from shed
- Local orientation
- General orientation
- Possible routes
- Means of obtaining money and clothes

At the time there was not much coherence of thought nor was there later but the seeking of information nevertheless proceeded apace. We had many wild ideas, one of which involved a mass breakout from the camp and a 'blitzkrieg' of sorts all the way home. I daresay whether that would have been successful too. Only those who can think of doing the impossible can achieve the impossible. If humans were not endowed with envisioning on gigantic scales then *impossible* would remain *impossible*.

The chief problem faced by us was opposition from amongst our own people. This was a very sorry state of affairs. It was of course quite clear that any attempt that would have to be made would be without the three senior officers present amongst us, unless of course there was a mass breakout. Their age stood in the way as a physical handicap. If an escape bid was attempted, they would simply have to be left behind. That was an unfortunate and a hard fact. Shah again was something else. During the first month he was with us in all that we were hoping to achieve, but after Malhotra's visit he joined the opposing camp and at one point, for sometime, even lured Sadiq away from us. His contention was that it was foolhardy on our part to even think about it and would invite the wrath of the Indians if they came to know that we were harbouring such thoughts. Maj. Iqbal was decidedly nervous about what would happen if the Indians came to know about our plans. Lt. Col. Khizer Hayat forbade us from attempting to escape because he did not consider it 'good behaviour'. We did not expect this kind of a reaction from him but in hindsight I put his obduracy down to fatherly concern for us. He probably felt that it would be a foolhardy act and may even result in the deaths of the attempting escapees. To calm Khizer Hayat's qualms, we told him that to get shot was an occupational hazard of our profession. During the period between 1972–1973 over 40 Pakistanis were shot dead by guards while they were 'attempting to escape', according to the Indians. More than 20 ultimately did mange to escape. I consider these deaths neither foolish nor futile. They gave up their lives for their nation's honour.

Despite all the untold hurdles that were building up by the day, our planning never came to a halt. But it did make our task more difficult. If the other inmates were thinking of the consequences that our escape would have upon them, then let them be aware of all that we were risking. When all the factors are weighed, balance is always heavier in favour of the escapees. Moreover, we were morally correct in our act, hence, whoever was thinking of themselves—to hell with them! Concern is appreciated but obstruction is unjustified and intolerable.

We got down to the acquirement of salient pieces of information from which would emerge our escape plan:

(a) **Layout of the camp.** This had to be studied in great detail and we had plenty of time. Since a detailed layout of the camp has been provided in a previous chapter, I will only highlight some salient features here. The area around these compounds within the outer wire was illuminated by spotlights. The portion of the camp outside the lighted perimeter remained entirely dark—the only lit up portion was the inside of the sheds. There was a high growth of elephant grass with numerous depressions in the area inside the outer wire. Only the grass growing in the OR compound had been pruned neatly. This was also true for the area along the wall. Stacks of cut grass were piled up at several places. The lights were focused in certain directions, which gave spotted shadow affect, the bulbs being of inferior quality. This was helpful for us. The barbed wire was tightly strung, hardly leaving any room for manoeuvring. All drains and depressions were effectively covered and blocked by bricks. These were periodically inspected by the Indian officers and JCOs to satisfy their security precautions. The area could only be affectively kept under surveillance if the sentries were continuously on the move since it was a large expanse to cover. Moreover, at night every sound magnified due to the deathly silence that prevailed. This was a factor that needed to be taken into consideration. The wall was quite high and there were only two gates. The main gate was guarded although the other iron gate which opened out into the unused railway line was unguarded. A number of trees were lined against the wall which would be of aid if required. The relief guard of sheds 1 and 7 slept next to the kote which was opposite the officer's compound. The Madrasis were good boys and took to sleeping early, with the result that there was virtually no movement in the area outside the prisoner's perimeter soon after it became dark. The only exception was when Scott or P.O. Singh would come occasionally and sleep over at the camp. After Singh went away, Scott's enthusiasm for his duty waned, hence, the surprise checks would take place once in a while. However the night of his duty would often occasion unwelcome surprise visits.

(b) Habits of sentries. Since more than two months had elapsed and not a single attempt or even a hint of an escape attempt had been made, one could feel the sense of complacency that had now come to prevail among the sentries. Some of them had come back from leave in the middle of June and for a fortnight or so they were very vigilant. After that they were apt to behave accordingly in relation to the type of guard commander who was on duty. Sentries would prowl inside the perimeter sometimes peering in through holes. Only one security light was left open in the officer's shed. Since jungle green is hard to discern at night, it would become quite difficult to place their exact location. The four regular guard commanders who were assigned in the month of July were categorized in accordance to their alertness:

(i) *Vigilant*. Naik Sundarasen was very friendly with me, giving us cigarettes and occasionally chatting with us. Nevertheless, he was very much on his toes and would awaken us while on duty often to check up on us. Moreover, he never slept when he was on duty and kept a watch on the sentries who would be forced to be extra vigilant. That he did not imbibe liquor was bad news for us, and when we confided in him that we would never think of escaping when he was on duty, we were not joking. Our night of escape had to be a 'non-Sundarasen' night. We had no doubt that he would have shot us as happily as he handed us cigarettes.

(ii) *Watchful*. Although Naik Pukhraj and Naik Thomas were good-natured and easy-going, they remained watchful. However they would not bother either us or their sentries too much. Though we could not find out for sure, we assumed that they both drank rum.

(iii) *Relaxed*. Naik Christopher would invariably be seen sleeping away soundly. He often had a glazed look about him—he definitely took a fair swig of rum occasionally. In his turn of duty, the sentries would squat and chat away. Rain usually provided a further dampener on their movements. Christopher was our best bet.

(c) **Means of exit from the shed.** Foremost to our plan was a silent break-out from the shed. We gave up the conventional idea of digging a tunnel very early on for various reasons. One, the water level was too high. Two, Indians would thoroughly check for any signs of tunnelling. They had probably read the same books that we had. The corners of the shed had a few outlets but thanks to my over-enthusiasm, stupidity and the effects of a raging storm, these outlets were soon spotted, cemented and bricked up from the outside. To add insult to injury, Uppal ordered us to keep them wet by throwing water on them for the cement to harden. Three, to unlock the doors and rolling them open would amount to ringing an alarm bell because of the noise that this would make. These tin sheds had probably been put up during the Second World War and were quite rusty. The only solution lay in contriving to open the bolts; holding down the tin sheets; and scrape through out of it on the appointed day. The tin sheets on the back door were also rusty and could be manipulated in time of need. We kept our possibilities open. The only problem was that the officers' shed remained under the nose of the sentries at night who patrolled at the back, and the guard commander in front, though there were always occasions when the watch would conveniently slacken: during the changing of the guards or when it was raining heavily. Hence, it had to be a silent operation. As regards opening of bolts at night would attract too much attention. To add to all this, Col. Khizer Hayat would not let us loosen the bolts during the day, thus, putting impediments in the smooth accomplishment of our plans. If Sadiq had been firmer with him, we would all have managed to escape.

(d) **Local orientation.** This was a very tricky subject. We had come to know at the very beginning that we were in Panagarh and this was probably the Engineers Supply Depot. We could see walls across the road, steel watch towers in the distance and hear enough railway shunting to guess that we were located in a fairly large Army Base. Malhotra had said that this camp had housed Polish detainees during the Second World War. But then Malhotra was prone to lying, however, this could have been true. The Station Commander, Brig. Coelho wore the crest of Artillery on his helic belt and the shoulder flash of the profile of the tiger on a red background. The troops who were guarding us were from the 203 Army Engineer Regiment. We got this information from a medical prescription chit. They belonged to 430 Field Company (from a notice board in Uppal's office). These troops were wearing the shoulder flash of a rising sun on a black background which we took to be that of the Indian Eastern Command and must have come from Madras. This was obviously originally a Madras Sapper and Miner unit. When Shah was taken to Calcutta, he had a mixed escort including a Lieutenant of Artillery.

The barber, Sep. Surinder Kumar, a talkative soul who was a Punjabi Hindu told us that he had been attached to the camp from a Light Aircraft Regiment. This confirmed the fact that Brig. Coelho was most probably the Commander of an Anti-Aircraft Brigade with the HQ and the best part of the Brigade here in Panagarh. Brig. Coelho had also said that he was in the vicinity of the Pathankot Airfield during the 1965 War. He had also read a news item about a suspected Naxalite arrested from one of the military schools in Panagarh. All this added up to the fact that Panagarh was a huge military base. Shah said that there were check posts on the roads leading into the camp, but slightly off the main roads. The sentries had told us that they had to watch movies in the Garrison Cinema because the town was far away. Shah calculated the distance of Calcutta at about 100 miles and Burdwan at about 30 miles. He couldn't decipher the milestones since they were written in Hindi. One of the sentries said that Asansol was about 30 miles to the west. We were worried about patrols outside the boundary walls and inside the cantonment at night. However no patrols were seen going from our camp outside the walls. We knew that at night at about 9.30 pm, civilian traffic outside the walls would slow to a trickle until 3 am when it picked up again. From the sounds of men and cattle, and of women and children playing in the fields we knew that there was a village immediately outside the camp.

Sep. Surinder Kumar asked me which *Riasat* (principality) was I a *Maharajkumar* (Prince) of. He said the Indian soldiers were gossiping that Sadiq Nawaz, Ayaz Mahmood, Amjad and I were most likely going to attempt an escape. That this was the subject of Indian '*langar gup*' (mess gossip) was a shock to us. We were revealing our plans in some manner—and we had to calm down in order not to attract attention or even speculation.

(e) General orientation. Newspapers, magazines and an appraisal of our general knowledge was the only way we could get a fair orientation of India. The newspaper was invaluable because it gave a fair idea of the general conditions prevailing inside India at the time. We came to know all about the curfews, disorder and the subsequent movements of the

Indian Army and the Police in various districts to enforce law and order. This was especially so after West Bengal had been placed under direct Presidential rule, with a corresponding increase of Naxalite activity. This placed certain areas literally out of bounds for us. Moreover, we became familiar with people's names, places and events. Such information is very helpful and builds up confidence when one is moving in unknown territory. News about continued American Aid to Pakistan resulting Indian reaction; the virtual house arrest of the Pakistan Deputy High Commission Staff in Calcutta; worsening Indo-Pak relations, all had a relative bearing upon our plans for escape. We used to minutely scrutinize the 'Letters to the Editor' section of the newspaper, in the hope of receiving some encrypted message from our people. From an article in the *Illustrated Weekly of India*, we obtained a complete map of India. This facilitated in furthering our knowledge of possible routes, distances and border areas. It would be impossible to recount the numerous clues that we collected, collated and disseminated. To give one example we even had a survey established of the percentage of Muslim population in various Indian states from a number of articles and features.

(f) **Possible routes.** Having calculated the distances from the map that was in our possession, the following possible alternatives were established:

(i) *Panagarh—Nepal Border.* Shortest route involved going via Raxaul through Assam and Patna, the distance working out to be approximately 300 miles. We did not know how the Nepalese authorities would be inclined to treat us. It would be very unfortunate if were handed back to the Indians. At that time I did not know as I know now that there were no passport/visa restrictions between India and Nepal, and we could have very well posed as Indians till we received help from the Pakistan Embassy. This route used to be Maj. Sadiq Nawaz's dream and he insisted that its safe negotiation would see us to freedom.

(ii) *Panagarh—East Pakistan.* Except for Maj. Sadiq Nawaz, all of us were inclined to forsake this route. We especially wanted to avoid Calcutta which was possible if we went north of Burdwan. The biggest drawback was the state of tension and conflict prevailing on the borders, leading us to conclude that they must have all been sealed by the Indian Army and the Border Security Force. Sadiq had one very wild proposal that we should get on board a foreign ship in Calcutta. Apparently a group of Pakistani army officers who escaped from Indian custody late in 1972 had come up with the same idea but later having reached Bombay dropped it as being too risky.

(iii) *Panagarh—Southern India.* Very long distances were involved in this but it gave us wide latitude of choosing direction of movement and port of exit. The biggest drawback was money and clothes, of which we were absolutely bereft.

(iv) *Panagarh—West Pakistan.* Again we were faced with the problem of long distances and the means of obtaining money from somewhere. Coupled with this fact was the movement of the Indian Army close to the borders. This virtually eliminated the Punjab border but we thought that we could get across the Rajasthan side after negotiating the desert. I would like to mention here that what we had excluded as not feasible, namely, the crossing of the Punjab borders was later done under fire by two commando officers after the 1971 War was over. That there was doubt about their credentials later was surprising, but then one of them was picked up a few years later because of his contacts with the Indian intelligence.

(g) Means of obtaining money and clothes. Acquiring clothes was the main problem because we had only green and white striped pyjamas and the cream bush-shirt jacket that had been issued to us by our benevolent captors. We couldn't really roam around in striped pyjamas because not only would they be a trifle too mod, they were not exactly the right type of fashion for escaped prisoners to sport. In such situations one likes to remain a little unobtrusive. We had a contingency plan to stitch white pyjamas out of our white bed sheets but this had to be a smooth and swift bit of tailoring just before the 'D Day'. I had been given a *lungi* (loin cloth) in Agartala Jail and I had badgered the Indians into giving back my *lungi* to use in place of a towel which they had not issued to us. This was particularly fortunate.

Money was the other problem. Naib Subedar Aurangzeb, who was in the other shed, had some Indian currency but he spent it all on cigarettes before we could relieve him of the cash. We needed money very badly. I had a couple of addresses from where we could obtain money but these were far away and in any case it was not a very definite proposition. One could always hijack money from wayfarers and Ayaz was very excited about doing this once we were safely outside the precincts of the boundary wall. I think all of us have the highwayman instinct in us to a great degree.

In any given situation, it is difficult to gauge a particular scenario where all the relevant factors will favourably combine to give us the optimum conditions required. A compromise has to be worked out with chance. God only helps those who help themselves. Faith in God is what human beings live with and that faith should instil in us a sense of purpose and determination, after which we must rely on our luck to get us across. We had to shake off the sense of complacency that was enveloping our existence. Simply being alive is not good enough—there must be a purpose to ones life. If we immerse ourselves in a state of self-satisfaction, no amount of inducement can later take us to any heights. Even extreme desperation will not be able to motivate us to escape and reach freedom. The Indians had us living in a fool's paradise regarding our impending departure, and we vacillated in judging whether it was the truth or a lie when the answer all along had been so simple: they had been lying to us all along. There was no deep philosophy involved here—the enemy must always be deceitful and cunning.

No plans can be made in the height of emotions. But more often than not, such is always the case—and they seldom succeed. However I am no one to preach this because I am often guilty of acting impulsively and am blamed for allowing my emotions to lead me. However, if one is guided by a singular deadly purpose, one is usually successful. Where there is something to be gained there is risk of something to be lost. Too often we do not execute our plans because we are afraid of the consequences. Moreover, we desire that everything must be perfect. However, in order to gain something, we have to take risks. A plan of escape carries with it the element of death. It is usually the 'fear of fear' which unnerves us. Often it is seen that once a plan is executed, fear fades into the background. But to fear is very human—in fact it is required in order to hold us back from behaving recklessly.

I have no hesitation in admitting that Sadiq Nawaz deserves the credit for my escape. He did most of the planning and it was he who kept me in control till the last moment. I was the one who managed to get away physically from the POW Camp; in actuality it was his escape that inspired me. Ayaz and Amjad also deserve credit—I was their representative who made it out to freedom.

I said goodbye to Uppal and his Madrasis on the evening of 16 July 1971.

I was praying that I should never see them again!

NOTE

1. Colonel Nusratullah was a soldier's soldier of the finest kind. Commissioned into 13th Lancers, he eventually commanded 23 Cavalry, remaining for many years as 'Colonel of the Regiment'. An unflappable soul who was tough as steel, he was in the first batch of commando officers trained in Cherat in 1957 by the US Special Forces to create the elite Special Services Group (SSG) of the Pakistan Army. An unassuming soul, Col. Nusrat specialized in teaching courses on 'Escape, Evasion and Survival', 'Stay-Behind Operations' etc. I consider myself fortunate to be his student.

   Our tutor-student relationship began in 1964, was nurtured in the late 1960s and cemented in 1970 (when I was flying a Aloutte-3 helicopter in Army Aviation). A superb teacher, he displayed utmost patience, although, he had no patience for fools.

8

ROAD TO CALCUTTA

All roads do not lead to Rome.

Of all the places to go to, one may ask, why Calcutta? Why indeed?

Many people whom I have had occasion to bore with the less lurid details of my narration from time to time have never really understood my reasons for making a beeline for Calcutta. Since my own assumptions really did not seem to be very valid at that time, one can understand their hesitation at not accepting my arguments in favour of taking the high road to the gay city of Calcutta.

Generally speaking, there were a few choices open to me: to either go north, south, east or west, and their variations thereof. The main GT Road was inclined more or less from east to west, running that is, from Calcutta to the Bihar region. From the north to the south, there was a vast expanse of the countryside which made headway in that direction almost impossible. The Indian anti-escape dragnet would have soon bagged me. To the west lay the Bihar region, with a fair percentage of Muslims, but one had to pass through the strike-ridden towns of Asansol and Durgapur. In their search for Naxalites, the Indian Army and police had sealed the area adjacent to the West Bengal-Bihar borders. In any case that would have been the first route the Indians would have laid a trap to nab me. In assessing my fellow POWs, I came to the conclusion that they would break under pressure—some earlier than later. Therefore as much as I detested my actions, I was bound to feed them the obvious: that I would head for the Bihar side where the language would not be a difficulty. And then I had to head in the opposite direction! To the west lay Calcutta, the vain hope was that I would get there in time to evade the subsequent roadblocks which would be set up to seal the area. Once the news of my escape was flashed to the law-enforcing authorities in the area I would be fair game for every Ram, Gopal and Bahadur Singh with an itchy trigger finger. An outside chance of succour existed in Calcutta City with its teeming population of unlawful elements. Try searching for a needle in a haystack! Moreover, I knew from my parents that Urdu was spoken very liberally in the city. The very size of that city had its charm—I could easily get lost there. Our escape committee, although, had maintained that heading towards Calcutta would be tantamount to foolishness. On the question of foolishness, who else could one have as a better candidate than me—I chose to go to Calcutta.

The city of Calcutta, in its vastness, would have afforded me comparatively open movement, without the fear of recognition. Even if the Indians were quick enough to sound an alert for me in the city, I would have merged easily among the cosmopolitan masses. To them it would have been the last priority to choose; the wrong place to go to. Hence, all factors considered, it was an unconventional choice for me to take. I decided to put the art of the unorthodox into practical implementation. Another reason for me to choose Calcutta was that it had a sizable population of Muslims and also some foreign missions from where one could expect to receive help—or so I hoped. The deciding factor was that I knew the address of a lady, one Zeenat Hamid by name. She had extended an invitation of sorts to me three years earlier, and for some reason, her address had remained in my memory, although the invitation was in fact no more than light-hearted formality, since when can Pakistani servicemen personnel go to India, even on a passport? The situation was quite abnormal, but boosted by supreme vanity and self confidence, I felt that there was an outside chance that she would recognize me.

I moved in the direction of Calcutta as soon as I got on to the main road. Since I was barefoot, it was quite difficult to traverse on the rough surface of the road. Though my feet were badly cut, I was as yet not feeling much pain. The lit up POW Camp was visible to the right. It seemed ominous and quiet, the threat of a siren going off at any moment ever present in my mind. This was the most dangerous part of my flight from Panagarh, because approximately a hundred or two hundred yards away to the left side of the road going towards Calcutta were military barracks (or offices). Sentries were present there, and I also passed a Quarter Guard. A board on the right indicated 'Military/ Police Check Post 100 Yards'. The arrow was pointing north. The road was completely deserted except for the occasional truck passing by. It was not prudent to take a lift there, neither was it advisable to start running and thereby attract attention. The only recourse left was to continue walking until I was away from that area and to hope that no one would notice. Since the road was open to public, I remained unobtrusive.

There were a number of railway crossings on that road. Railway shunting was going on inside a walled camp on the left side, probably the main Engineer Supply Depot Camp. At one of the crossings, almost outside the camp's periphery, I noticed that the trucks would slow down as they crossed over. A truck with a spare tyre jutting out from the back slowed down. I went over to one side and kept watching. As soon as I got a chance, I grabbed at the tyre and hurled myself onto the truck, grabbing the ropes which had been used to tie down the cargo. We travelled for a considerable distance until we approached habitation. I must have remained on the truck for at least twenty minutes and the distance that we travelled was probably eight to ten miles. It would have been unwise to press my luck further. I jumped off the truck as soon as it slowed down. The distance between me and the camp was now quite substantial, although, it had hardly been an hour since I had reached the road. Since no truck was going to stop in the night, no matter which country one may be in, hence, it was no use my trying to flag one for a lift. Moreover, because of the prevailing Naxalite trouble in West Bengal, it was not sensible. The traffic by now had thinned down to a trickle.

Time had come to start my run/walk drill. In the Army, 'RWR' (Run, Walk, Run) is known to be the favourite form of exercise for artful dodgers, only exceeded by the 'Sarkari Double'. The term RWR is also known as 'Running Without Reason'. In my case I certainly had reason, but performing this exercise when one's feet are cut may not be the ideal pastime one may imagine it to be. To add insult to injury, the state of the road in that stretch was simply atrocious: not only did the road need repair; the surface was also uneven. Due to the rain and its hygroscopic effect, no immediate effects were felt on my feet, but I frequently had to get on to the sides of the road that was muddy to get some relief for my feet which slowed my flight considerably. The bad patches, combined with the sharp stones really played merry hell with the soles of my feet. I consoled myself by freely cursing the contractors for being crooks and cheats in failing to keep that road in proper order. One can excuse them on the grounds of ignorance, because after all how were they to know that I would be carrying out an inspection of their roads with my bare feet in such meticulous detail. However one does wish that the Grand Trunk (GT) Road which was built by Sher Shah Suri and improved upon by the British could at least have been kept in reasonable shape by the Indians. I believe it is now a four-lane two-way highway.

To the left of the road, at a distance, trains could be seen periodically passing, making me think about other options other for my bleeding feet. Surprisingly, the trains were moving silently, without making any sound. It took me a while before I realized that they were electric trains.

My first goal was to reach Burdwan. It was imperative that I cross Burdwan before the search for me was commenced. We had estimated Burdwan to be approximately 35 to 40 miles away. It was not possible for me to reach this distance by daybreak without taking a ride. Nevertheless I pressed on doggedly. The initial flush of having accomplished Phase 1 and 2 successfully was now wearing off and I was feeling very tired. Having crawled for nearly 400 yards, though mostly on leopard crawl because of the high grass, I was now gradually beginning to feel the effects. But this was no test or practice. It would have been fatal to tarry and rest my body. Life itself is a great incentive and can drive man to great heights. In one's desire to remain alive, the body is willing to endure tremendous amounts of torture. I was under no illusions as to what the Indians would do to me if they ever caught up with me again.

It was raining softly, the raindrops trickling down my face; the atmosphere was quite cool. My greatest worry was that my legs would give way—it had been a long while since they had been exercised for such a long stretch. I was racing against time, my only thought at the time being to cover maximum distance between myself and Panagarh before daybreak. That was when my escape would be discovered. The only way for me was to continue with my walk/run routine.

The camp sheds would be opened at 5 am. Only the gates were rolled open but they were not unlocked. A few minutes later, tea would be brought in a bucket. We had to go up to the wire to collect our cup of tea. The man who brought the tea would impatiently call out a few times before going over to the next shed. In effect, he was supposed to be accompanied by a sentry but this practice was often ignored. If the guard commander did not suspect why I was not coming out as usual, the next check was after half an hour or so, at 6 am, when the roll call was taken. Keeping in mind the time spent in discovery; the following confusion; local investigation; and then finally passing the gathered information to the Camp Commandant, I could safely calculate that it would be 7 am by the time the actual search orders were sounded outside the camp. Even then it was just possible that the local Station

Details of Panagarh
Camp Location in India

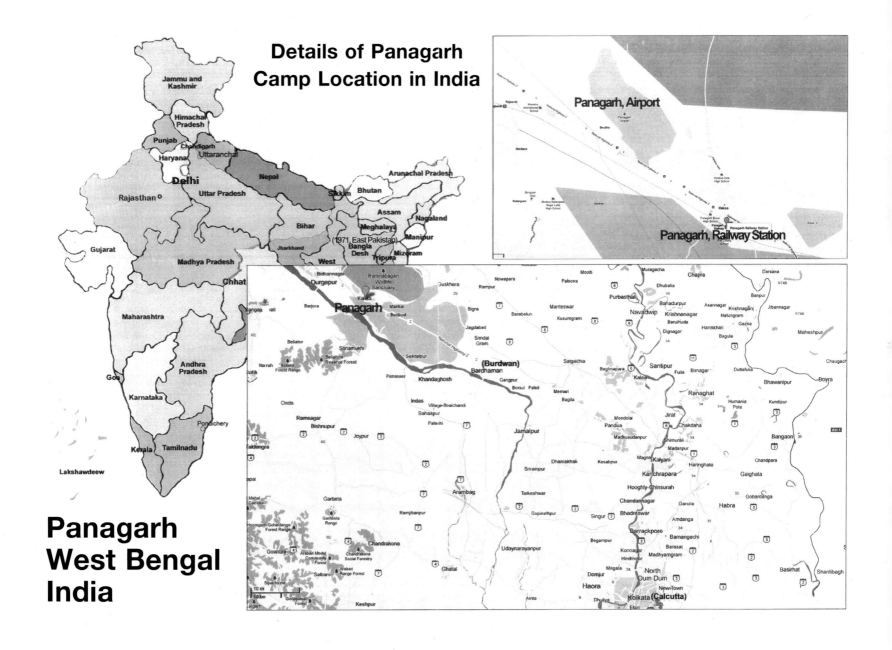

Panagarh, Airport

Panagarh, Railway Station

Panagarh
West Bengal
India

Northern India and Nepal

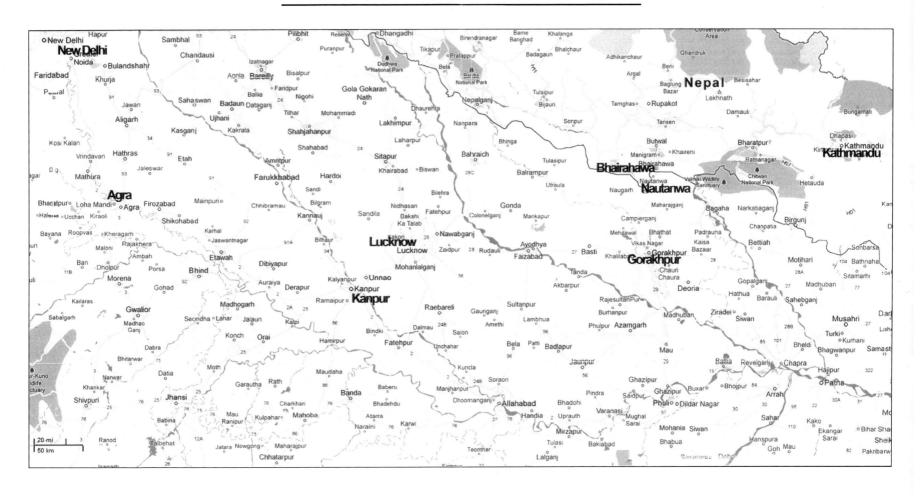

Commander decided to conduct a quick local search before informing the authorities all over for a general alert. After all, he was the one responsible and this could cost him dearly. Hence I gave myself a clear run till 7.30 am. Not a very perfect way to calculate time and space but in the circumstances the best possible. Moreover, having observed Indian red-tapism in action in the camp, I was actually not inclined to have a very high opinion of the inherent bureaucracy in their standard operating procedure. There was bound to be hesitation in breaking the 'bad' news to all concerned. It would also require a man of rare qualities to actually order an 'all out alert' without consulting the higher powers that are. I was hoping that the Indian Army would react as any other large bureaucratic set up. However, my plans had to proceed according to what I could have accomplished (having been trained in the Pakistan Army) and not rely on how hopelessly the Indians would perform. One had to plan for the worst and hope for the best.

As I walked on, I began to pass occasional wayside stalls and restaurants meant as truck stops. I had to be careful while crossing such places and walk as casually as possible in order not to draw attention. At one place I had the misfortune of attracting the undue attention of village dogs but I remembered that I should not display any fear. To have dealt with them would have been quite tragic and not at all desirable.

It must have been around 3 am that I reached a town by the name of Jalsi. Here I made another attempt to swing onto a truck that came by, but it was dangerous and futile and I gave up the idea. As I was resting for a while on a culvert, I saw a signpost with 'Railway Station' written on it. I got off the main road and headed towards it. Having heard about freight trains, hobos and ticket-less travel, it was not out of place to try my luck. The old brick road leading to the station was terrible and tortuous on my feet. When I reached the railway station, I asked a sleepy character when the next train to Burdwan would arrive but he could not provide me with a clear answer. However after some delay he managed to tell me that it would come around 8 am. I had no option but to continue with my walk on the main road—having wasted a good deal of time. As I was making my way back, I saw a patrol of four men in khaki coming along the railway line to the railway station. It was becoming lighter by the minute and the sun would soon be out. Though quite tired by now, a sense of urgency kept me going. Morning meant the discovery of my escape and the loss of freedom of my movement on the main road. It was imperative for me to keep moving in order to ensure maximum distance between the camp and myself by 7 am. The pain on the soles of my feet was excruciating by now—it was only God's will that kept me going. My legs were moving listlessly, almost involuntarily, my greatest fear being that I was far behind the race as regards time. I simply had to get clear.

My first requirement was money which I did not have. Where was I to get it? For some time I deluded myself with the prospect of selling my bush shirt, but one look at my arms and shoulders in the morning light made me change my mind. I would attract too much attention with all the cuts and bruises, given of course if the bush shirt managed to get sold.

What does a man think about in such circumstances even if one is a hopeless dreamer? My thoughts were of money, clothes, cars, the comforts of home and of my country. As my body fatigued, the reasoning of my mind tended to become more and more pessimistic. But this feeling had to be shaken off; it could be fatal for me. Complacency and pessimism are not for a man in flight. The only resort was to repeat the *Kalima* over and over which provided solace to my heart. I thanked God to have brought me this far. He could not forsake me at this juncture—it was now up to me to justify His kindness—I had to continue to endure the physical strain.

By about 6 am, I was exhausted. Even though I had been moving continuously all night, I was still short of Burdwan. Calcutta seemed millions of miles away and I needed to rest. A culvert afforded a place for me to sit down. Trucks had started to go past in increasing numbers. People were perched on the loads at the back and I looked forlornly at them. Half heartedly I kept trying to thumb a ride but without any luck.

I had prepared a story from this moment onwards:

I was Mahboob Murtaza, a Bihari Muslim born in Dhanbad, and was employed as a servant in the house of Zeenat Hamid of 8, Royt Road, Calcutta. My hometown was Lucknow. My parents were supposed to be old family servants of Zeenat Hamid's father. Zeenat Bibi had come to Calcutta recently to work in a firm. I had gone to Lucknow to see my ailing mother and was robbed of all my belongings on the way back, including money. Hence from Asansol onwards, I had to travel on foot.

Though I had never been to Calcutta, I tried to make my story as plausible as possible. In actuality, my birth place was also Dhanbad hence I could speak with confidence. I repeated this story to myself so many times that by now I myself was convinced that I was actually a servant of Zeenat Bibi. Of course if anybody had really started questioning me, he could have punched big holes in my story. But that was a chance that I had to take. I was looking forward to meeting Zeenat in Calcutta.

While I was sitting in the culvert, I saw an army truck approaching from the right, from the direction of Panagarh. There goes the ball game, I thought. Sheer helplessness swept through me, replaced almost immediately by an urge to run for it. But to make any hasty move was to attract attention. I resigned myself to sit there and hope for the best. I watched it come closer. The truck was a faded green Mercedes Benz— and had four civilians sitting in it—all in the front seat. I was able to gauge all this while the truck was still a good hundred yards away. Not wasting any time, I signalled the truck to stop. Lo and Behold—it rolled on for about a hundred yards and then stopped. I ran up to it, told the men sitting inside that I had been robbed, and pleaded with them to give me a lift till Burdwan. A man in a *dhoti* (loin cloth), with a marked Bihari accent inquired what my final destination was. I told him that I wanted to go to Calcutta but had no money. He laughed and asked me to climb in at the back, and assured me that he would take me all the way up to Calcutta. I scrambled aboard and established myself in the corner of the left side since there was no tailboard. I then took stock of the situation.

This was a piece of luck in its most blatant form. The back of the truck was empty except for some iron/tin pieces which were obviously part of the truck in better days. The floor of the truck was entirely covered with rust. Whatever was left of the canvas tarpaulin was rolled up and was flapping in my face so that I had to tie it all over again. The truck was really swaying and rattling in an ungainly fashion but that did not worry me in the least. I had a car like that once. The four people who were crammed together in the front were in high spirits. Three of them were Biharis and only one, the driver was Bengali. For a mile or so I watched the scenery and thought about this fabulous piece of luck that had come my way. Luck had seemed to be overflowing in my direction since the previous night. It was as if God had placed these good Samaritans in my path on purpose and I cannot thank Him enough. I shudder when I think of the circumstances and the corresponding chain of good luck.

I could feel the fresh breeze and light raindrops on my face. It was very freshening. Fatigue seeped through me and I slept fitfully. A jolt woke me up. We had come into a town. The road sign proclaimed it to be Burdwan. It was not until I came back to freedom to Pakistan and was able to take a look at the map that I realized that I had covered slightly more than 20 miles. Until that time, I had thought that I only covered 15 or 16 miles distance from the camp. Since all the milestones were in Hindi; it was Greek to me.

While we were passing by a traffic island a policeman signalled us to stop. The driver took out some documents and got off the truck to meet the policeman. The owner of the truck, a Bihari Hindu, and his friend walked halfway down the street and seemed quite agitated about something. The mechanic and I began to chat. He was a Bihari Muslim and I repeated my 'cock and bull story' to him. The mechanic was quite sympathetic and ensured me that they would take me all the way to Calcutta. I asked him why they were stopped, and why did they look agitated? I was told that the Bihari Hindu had bought the truck from an army depot in Panagarh. Since he had begun to drive it immediately, it was not yet registered under civilian registration and that they were going to do that in Calcutta. The only hitch in this story was that if the policemen cared to look at the licence plate carefully, he would have realized that it was a civilian one! The Bihari Hindu was obviously prepared for the consequences of the risk. After some haggling, there was an exchange of money and we parted company from this erstwhile guardian of law. Hardly had we driven a distance of 200 yards, that we were again stopped by policemen at the entrance of a road bridge. Having thus complied with the formalities thus entailing, we proceeded on. We did not go too far, at the other end of the bridge—some more policemen were waiting.

All this while I sat huddled in the back trying to look casual and unconcerned, and managing to feel all the more conspicuous. Even a cursory suspicion on their part would have landed me back in the pen. Hence I was not going to take the chance of even looking towards them for long. My heart remained beating firmly, if a trifle hurriedly. The third squad of 'tax collectors' left the driver without the usual salute, since this time he protested firmly against doling out more bribe.

We moved on. Huddled at the back, I soon dozed off again and would occasionally wake up when passing some habitation or railway crossing. We were on the road to Calcutta. The countryside extended on both sides—green and laden with crops—and wet with rain. The railway line, with its overhead electric cables remained in view. It kept drizzling incessantly. My bush shirt served as an adequate pillow under my head. I had covered my feet with mud to hide my cuts and bruises. I was certain that by now my escape must have been discovered.

Between snatches of sleep, I watched the road being left behind and raised my head to see the road ahead. We eventually stopped at a roadside stall, and I was offered tea and eatables by my hosts, which I gratefully accepted. The stall's owner, a very fat Sikh, spoke in a strange mixture of Punjabi, Urdu and Bengali. As I was washing my face, I saw an army vehicle full of officers go tearing by towards the west. The Bihari Hindu became interested in hearing the story of my misfortune. He also asked me about my final destination. He seemed quite touched at my condition and told me not to worry, and that we would soon be in Calcutta. He knew where Royt Road was; it being very close to Park Street where they were going. I did not want to arouse their curiosity too much hence I kept my conversation to an absolute minimum lest I talk my way into trouble. My ignorance of local conditions was too pronounced to be displayed in all its bliss. It was a curious juxtaposition of affairs. I accepted a cigarette from the mechanic and puffed at it, forgetting that I did not smoke. Soon I was coughing as all who do not smoke do.

We were stopped twice more for the doling out of the usual bribes: once at an Octroi post, and once when a Highway Patrol stopped us. After the usual haggling, the Bihari Hindu would hand over the requisite amount. It is a novel thing for a man to witness the exchange of bribe.

Finally, while we were nearing Calcutta we were again stopped by the police. It seemed my benefactors had taken an unauthorized route. We turned left and stopped about 50 yards on. The usual fare changed hands and I saw a Boeing aircraft on its take-off leg. One jeep and a dodge stopped at the crossroads and set up a road block. The rest of the convoy sped in the direction that we had come from. As we were pulling away, I saw that the sentries at the roadblock had stopped a bus and were scrutinizing the passengers. To me it was clear and I was not being paranoid: not only was the general alarm out for me, the powers-that-be in Eastern Command were now looking at Calcutta as a possible destination for the one that had 'gotten away'.

We entered the outskirts of Calcutta. From my geography lesson in Class 3 I had learnt that Calcutta was the third largest city in the world. What they had forgotten to mention was that it was also the most dingy city of the world at that time. Those who label Karachi as a dirty city have certainly not seen Calcutta—had they done so—they would not have survived a visit to Calcutta in 1971. (I am given to understand by my friends who live and work in Calcutta that it is very different now.) An endless row of shabby housing could be seen alongside the road. We came to a dirty river, crossed a dirty bridge—and finally we were on the Barrackpore Road. There was a continuous din of traffic and hustle-bustle. It would take me a while before I got used to the 'big city' atmosphere again. The big and tall buildings that I had imagined were nowhere in sight. All one could see were people carrying black umbrellas, riding on black bicycles, or in automobiles, most of them black in colour. Helmetted police in riot and wireless vans were seen roaming all over. One could almost sense the state of anarchy and violence—the wireless mesh on the police vehicles symbolizing that it was all the better to keep grenades and home made bombs away. My mother's eyes had seen Calcutta more than thirty years earlier. I stored this sight away in my memory to tell her that the Calcutta that she knew and talked about did not resemble the Calcutta I saw on 17 July 1971. In a way it was most disappointing. There is such a vast difference in what we imagine and visualize and then see for ourselves.

We came to a small workshop which was at the end of the road. I got off and after thanking the Bihari Hindu, I began to walk away. But he stopped me and told me that since I was comparatively new in Calcutta, he should better give me some directions. To get to Royt Road, one had to catch a tram close to the bridge which was adjacent to the workshop, then from there to Naya Ali Mohallah Mor, and subsequently get onto Tram No. 20 which would take me to Park Street. He took out a rupee and gave it to me. I was shocked but he smiled at me and said: 'You do not have anything on you and you have to get home somehow.' I did not possess adequate words to thank him.

I walked away from the workshop. My limbs were stiff with the residual fatigue and the concrete road pierced into my feet that were throbbing with pain. It would take some time to get used to it.

I was way ahead of my schedule and adrift in Calcutta with a rupee in my pocket, for better or for worse. The mirage of freedom was gradually solidifying into reality.

A destitute optimist was at large in Calcutta City.

9

OH CALCUTTA!

Calcutta,[1] the anglicized name of Kolkata as it is now known, is located on the east bank of the Hooghly River. It is the capital of West Bengal and the cultural capital of India. The English East India Company had arrived here in AD 1690.

I had met Zeenat Hamid at one of the picnics organized by friends at Rangamati which is located in the Chittagong Hill Tracts. She had come from Calcutta to visit relatives in Chittagong. Zeenat and I entered into a conversation about Calcutta. I was particularly interested because my maternal grandmother who, although, belonged to Midnapore which is located in the South of Calcutta, had been brought up in Calcutta. Most of my mother's schooling was done in Calcutta. They lived at Park Circus.

I met Zeenat at parties twice again where she jokingly suggested that if ever we 'invaded' Calcutta, I must make it a point to visit her. She lived on 8, Royt Road. She was insistent that I jot her address down in my diary—it has stuck in my memory ever since.

On the day that I reached Calcutta, i.e., 17 July 1971, I made a beeline for her house hoping against hope that she would be there. With supreme vanity I decided that she was sure to recognize me. Since she was a non-Bengali, I was hoping for a reaction of revulsion on her part, at the killings of non-Bengalis in Chittagong, some of whom could well be her relatives. This thought made the prospect of her coming to my aid a distinct possibility.

Following the guidance of the Bihari Hindu and with one rupee in my pocket, I took the tram to the given address. When I reached, I was in for a shock. House Number 8 turned out to be a tailor's shop—had been for many years! I freely cursed Zeenat Hamid and consigned her to all corners of Hell. She had completely misled me. However I could not afford to waste any time over her and had to quickly rethink my course of action.

Going to the Pakistan Deputy High Commission was out of the question. From the newspapers I had gathered that the Deputy High Commissioner and most of his staff had defected and had joined the Bangladesh government that had been set up in exile in Calcutta, and the ones that were still at the Chancery were virtually prisoners. To try and contact them would be tantamount to putting my neck in the noose. My only hope rested with the mission of a Pakistan-friendly country. For some time I searched for some Arab or Muslim mission but could not find any. The other alternative for me was to go to the US Consulate. From an advertisement that I had read in a newspaper, I remembered that it had recently shifted to Shakespeare Sarani, wherever that may be. It was reasonable to assume that the other consulates were also located in the same vicinity. I had to exercise extreme caution. I looked quite decrepit and I did not want to arouse any suspicion. Therefore I had to be very careful while asking for directions. I finally managed to reach the US Consulate, recognizing the 'Stars and Stripes' on top of a building. Police vans were parked outside. After a desultory search for some other diplomatic mission, I decided to seek help from the Americans.

It is important to discuss why I ever thought that I could get help from the Americans, in fact, I convinced myself that if I asked them for help I would get it. Before one seeks succour from anybody in such adverse circumstances, one must have faith in that somebody. I have been asked by several people as to why did I place so much hope and faith in the Americans, even at the peril of my life? A fugitive has usually nothing left except hope. His faith can lay a solid base for even an inkling of hope to snowball into an avalanche. To have that trifling amount of faith, a person must be aware of certain facts or conditions. My answers arouse suspicion in the minds of those who get themselves enmeshed in conspiracy theories. I have been repeatedly and pointedly asked this question, and to some I can never provide them with a satisfactory answer. My reasoning was based on my intimate knowledge of the Americans and all my evaluations stemmed from that. It was not based on chance alone and my appreciation turned out to be completely accurate. Forty years later I have no reason to change my mind. Although as the saying goes: 'it was a near run thing!'

I started my education in an American Convent in Comilla, my first teachers being Sister Mary Leo and Sister Mary Joan of Arc. I remained in the hostel from 1953 (with an interval of a couple of years) as a boarder till 1958. They were the first Americans I knew and all my subsequent impressions stem from them. They taught me the value of leading an ethical life. Most of all they never interfered with the teachings of my own religion, Islam. I love them for their goodness and because they never attempted to influence my thinking. For this I can never forget them or thank them enough. From them I received lessons which could not be rendered to me by a thousand books. Their guidance gave me the strength to think for myself.

It has become fashionable in the recent past to criticize anything American. The fact remains that the American taxpayer doles out a lot of hard earned cash for the benefit of the poorer nations of the world. We unfortunately come in that category and in times of any calamity that we may face, they are among the first to come to our aid. But we have always received (and still do) an unfavourable reaction from the US press. Most Muslim nations do. Nevertheless the US Government has given us moral and material support during times of our dire need and it does not behove us to be ungrateful.

During that particular period, there were frequent demonstrations in front of the American Consulate General daily and President Nixon's effigy was burnt every other day. It did not need a deep study of human psychology to reach the conclusion that the Americans in the Consulate General in Calcutta would not be favourably disposed towards the Indians. Not that they were waiting to embrace wayward vagrants like me with merry abandon, but there did exist a distinct possibility that they would not be very averse to Pakistanis.

I assessed that my primary goal was to get entry inside the Consulate premises and start talking—let the Americans worry about me after that. But getting into the Consulate was the main problem. Like a true soldier, I did extensive reconnaissance of all the routes leading to my target. But all entry points leading towards it had been covered by the police. A park near the Netherlands Consulate provided me a place to sit down and consider the various possibilities and routes. But after examining the area, I realized that there was no way that I could reach it since the police had not left any opening unguarded.

As time went on and evening approached I became more and more aware of the hopelessness of my situation. I was outside an important transit point and there was no way of getting inside.

About a mile away from the US Consulate, I came across an elderly American couple. From the number of cameras that they were carrying, they looked like tourists. I was desperate and they seemed to me to be the only way out of my impasse. I thought of the possibility of approaching them for help. It was nearly 5 pm and people were streaming home from work. I thought that I had a good chance of passing unnoticed if I contacted them now. With my heart in my mouth, I went up to the couple and politely asked them to inform someone at the American Consulate that I required help. The couple nearly collapsed at the Oxford English coming out of the mouth of one in tatters. I was conscious of the curious stares of passers by. The couple flatly refused. By now I was desperate and my anxiousness was visible on my face. I pleaded with them that if they did not help me, I had a fair chance of getting killed. After mulling over for a while, they asked me to follow them. Of all the places, they took me to the Salvation Army. As we approached it, I saw a number of Indians in the compound. Thanking the couple profusely, I begged to be let off. I had no intentions of being salvaged by the Salvation Army. Nevertheless I was grateful to them for trying to help me out.

As evening time approached in Calcutta, a kind of frenzy built up. Everyone was hurrying home. I realized that this was because Calcutta was not a very safe place to be out at night. Because of the Naxalite trouble and the refugees from East Pakistan, a curfew was in force. The approaching dusk increased my urgency of getting help soon. I could not risk being picked up on the road at night, either by the Naxalites or by the police. A crescendo of urgency and panic was rising in me—I had to take action fast.

The police were everywhere. There was a small Post Office about 300 yards from the American Consulate. Only one hope remained in my mind. I would have to ask them for help on the phone. Being in native clothes, it was a risk to approach the Post Office—but it was a risk that had to be taken. Trying to look as inconspicuous as possible, I walked into the Post Office. The clerk at the counter threw a bored look in my direction. There was a telephone booth with a directory lying next to it in the corner. A number of people were waiting for his attention. I started to leaf through the pages of the directory, but was not able to find the US Consulate's number anywhere in either 'C' or 'U'. I could not risk going up to the clerk to ask him for information. Almost giving up, it suddenly dawned on me that I should look under 'A'. Sure enough, it was there, bold and clear. I literally dived into the telephone booth and dialled their number. The clerk in the meantime had left his seat and had gone somewhere, which was just as well, because had he been present, he would have been shocked at what I was saying.

A US Marine Sergeant answered the call. I had rehearsed what I would say to him. I told him that I was a Pakistan Army Officer and had escaped from an Indian Army Prison Camp; that I needed help badly; and that if I was caught, I would be shot by the Indians. I give the US Marine full marks for his quick response. He identified himself as Sgt. Frank Adair,[2] and asked me where I was at the moment. I told him that I was quite near the American Consulate but could not enter because of the heavy police cover. I asked him if he could send a car out to get me, but he replied that there was no transport available at the moment, although, he told me, whatever needed to be done, had to be done fast. He was sure that the telephones were tapped. After a brief pause, he said that he was willing to walk up to the Post Office—was I willing to walk back in with him? I said that I was.

An odd sense of unreality seemed to sweep through me as I came out of the Post Office and took up position near the corner to wait for Sgt. Adair. Suddenly it seemed too simple—I was inclined to disbelieve that it had really happened.

Would I manage to get through the cordon?

Were the Indians already aware that I was in Calcutta and was trying to get inside some foreign mission?

Would they have alerted their intelligence agencies for such an eventuality?

But the thought of my seeking help from the Americans must have been far from their minds. As I waited patiently for Sgt. Adair, I was overcome with a sudden sense of calm and confidence. I was a little nonplussed at the speed of reaction of the US Marine.

At the corner across from where I was standing, a 'sit-down' strike was in motion by the employees of some firm against a 'lock-out'. I walked a little away from them so that I was more visible and waited on the pavement. Dusk had fallen and it had grown reasonably dark. Finally, I saw an American, a tough looking chap of medium height walking towards me. I went up to join him in the darkness so that we would not be noticed by prying eyes while we spoke to each other.

'Sergeant Frank Adair?' I ask him.

He looked at me in surprise, taken aback at my appearance. He murmured that I spoke excellent English for the state that I was in, and asked me if I had the courage to walk in with him. I looked at him but did not reply. We started walking towards the Consulate.

The pavement was wet with rain. I was barefoot. Although we only needed to cover a short distance, it seemed like a thousand yards.

Nobody noticed us but as we began to cross the last road leading to the Consulate, all eyes seemed to turn towards us. My heart was beating loudly. With abated breath, we crossed over through the cordon. At the gate one of the Embassy Guards stepped in front of me but only for a moment. A word and a glance from Sgt. Adair made him step back. We were in through the gate. The time was approximately 6 pm. I let out a deep sigh of relief. Although I was still far away from home, at least I had reached my first sanctuary.

NOTES

1. The word Calcutta has its roots in *Kalikata*, the name of one of the villages in the area. Job Charnock, an administrator with the English East India Company is credited for founding the city. The British built the Fort William in 1702. It was used as a regional base to station British troops.

   It is interesting to note that in the 1970s Calcutta was almost 80 per cent communist. There was the Communist Party Leninists, Communist Party Marxist, and the Communist Party Marxist-Leninists. Then there were the Naxalites. None of the parties got along with each other.

2. I spent many years trying to locate Sgt. Frank Adair. Ultimately, during the visit of the US Special Envoy for Pakistan and Afghanistan, Richard Holbrooke's visit to Islamabad, I mentioned my Calcutta episode to one of the military members of his team, Lt. Gen. John Allen of the US Marines, who was then Deputy Commander Central Command. He went out of his way to trace out Frank for me. John Allen took the trouble of ringing me from Tampa where he was based and gave me Frank's telephone number. Frank who was in Los Angeles was expecting my call. When I called him up, we chatted as if the barrier of four decades had not come in between us. Frank had joined the Los Angeles Police Department in 1972.

10

AMERICAN AID: 1971 STYLE

Frank Adair took me straight to a small room inside the US Consulate General. In the light, he took a good look at me—told me to stay put and went out. It was a small room full of books and papers, obviously an office. I hardly had time to look around when Frank was back, bringing with him a bottle of antiseptic, band aid and a bowl of water. A very pretty American girl who I saw sitting at the telephone switchboard counter glanced in. Frank Adair closed the door on her face. He informed me that someone would be there in a short while to talk to me—till then I had to sit tight.

From the moment we exchanged our first words, I had begun to like Frank Adair. He must have been a few years younger than me. I had reasons to believe at that time that this instant bonding between us was mutual. I was not mistaken. Frank Adair's role was central in my quest for freedom which I can never forget or be grateful enough. We were simply two young men: one an American and the other a Pakistani, brought together by a quirk of fate and with nothing in common but the unspoken bond of camaraderie between soldiers. To him I must have looked like a loafer off the streets. Perhaps what I liked most about him was that he asked me no questions and was not intrusive. He must have guessed my condition—that I was already overwhelmed with apprehension and tension—also, that I would soon be doing a great deal of talking on the subject. In his own way, his confident demeanour exuded a sense of protectiveness and that more than anything alleviated my fears. I was acutely aware of the multiple cuts and bruises on my body which seemed to suddenly come alive. The wounds could be salved by medicine, but my morale was bolstered by the tremendous expression of support that I saw in his eyes.

After about ten minutes, a bespectacled gentleman who introduced himself as Charles Coudert[1] breezed in clutching a brief case. He asked me to follow him to another room on the first storey where he heard me out in detail. Our session lasted for 30 to 40 minutes, at the end of which I made a formal request for my safe journey back to Pakistan. I told him that if that was not possible then I should be granted 'political asylum'. He patiently explained to me that I was not eligible for 'political asylum'. I then asked for some time to recuperate, some clothes and financial help which would be more in the form of a repayable loan. Coudert's attitude at first was cold and uncompromising. He told me that under the prevailing circumstances the Americans could not help me. The most he could do was to give me some money which would suffice for a few meals; that too from his own pocket. His contention was that I would simply have to walk out of the Consulate just the way I had come in. Like hell I was going to! It was quite an impasse.

Coudert had gone out of the room a number of times to consult somebody higher up. Although I had no way of knowing, I had the feeling that our conversation was being monitored elsewhere. I realized that I would have to press him harder to get results out of him and told him that I was very disappointed at the Americans for turning me out to be killed by the Indians. I said if I were to meet the fate they had in store for me, I might as well make it worth my life. I requested that if I were forced out of the diplomatic sanctuary, I would like to call a Press Conference to inform the world about Indian interference in East Pakistan, with both weapons and soldiers, details of which I just happened to know a great deal about. Since I would be shot by the Indians in any case, this was the only way to make sure that my death was of some benefit to my country. I also insisted that I be allowed to talk to the Pakistan High Commissioner in New Delhi on telephone. I regret if my tirade sounded like blackmail, but it was the only way I could get some results. It seemed to work! Charles Coudert was nonplussed for a while. Americans do not like to appear as being insensitive in such matters—it goes against their tradition. I may have sounded rather too melodramatic but the hard fact did remain that the Indians had a great stake in seeing me silenced in one way or the other, that is if they ever got hold of me. I was a living witness to the direct interference of the Indians in the internal affairs of Pakistan. Moreover, I had escaped from their covert top security POW Camp and hence was an embarrassment to them. The Indians would have given a lot to shut me up permanently. I am afraid that I did put it across to the Americans rather too bluntly but I had no choice. I love my country; I also love my life. Life is one possession that one does not give up too easily. There must be a worthwhile return for it and I was willing to resort to drastic means to preserve it.

Charles Coudert, obviously taken aback by my seeming determination for a 'hara-kiri', bustled off to consult somebody again. When he returned he had a hint of a smile on his face and I knew that I had turned some corners. He informed me that although I should not get my hopes up, I was to be provisionally accepted as a 'guest', pending further decision from the 'people' concerned. I learnt later that this involved the US Secretary of State and the American Ambassador in New Delhi and Islamabad. I was coming up in the world—a far distance from the penniless vagrant of the morning. Although I knew that I still had a long way to go, somehow I was certain that the situation was going to get better. An immense wave of relief swept through me.

At that time I had no knowledge of Henry Kissinger's clandestine visit to China through Pakistan's good offices. This had been arranged personally by General Yahya Khan only a few days earlier. The United States, Pakistan and China had gone to great lengths to keep the historic opening to China a secret. This included the subterfuge that Kissinger was sick and recuperating in Nathiagali. It was a decisive shift of US policy. Nixon opening to China tilted the strategic balance—the profound impact it had forty years later was still very much a mirage in 1971. There was euphoria in the US about the success of Kissinger's visit and a good deal of gratitude was lavished on Yahya Khan and Pakistan who acted as the facilitator as well as the conduit.

As luck would have it my timing was perfect. With these new developments taking place, even though I was not at all aware of them at the time, there was no way the Americans were not going to help me. The discussions of the officers at the US Consulate centred around how they could help me while remaining within the diplomatic parameters and which would not make them vulnerable to Indian allegations. Many years later, I accosted Henry Kissinger during the Annual Summit at the World Economic Forum in Davos and reminded him of the help given to me by the Americans. From his blank expression, and after repeating my story twice, it was clear to me that he did not remember it—or it could be that he was never brought into the loop. I felt quite deflated but then Kissinger was known to be self-centred and dismissive.

I was to stay overnight in the Chancery Building, and was taken to the US Marine Detachment offices where my friend Frank helped me to settle down on a sofa. I put my feet up on the table. After some time he brought some food and I quietly celebrated my father's birthday which was that day, i.e., on 17 July 1921—fifty years ago. I knew that he would be feeling down since celebrating birthdays together meant a great deal to us. I worried for his wellbeing.

However I shook off the feeling of despondency that had suddenly enveloped me. With a growing sense of self assurance, I was certain that the Americans were going to help me. They had already gone too far to back off now. As the subsequent events unfolded my faith in them was justified. Charles Coudert was an intelligence operative all the way through—a man who did not expose his emotions. He was cold and calculating, and certainly didn't care whether I lived or died. To him I was only someone from whom he could extract information. I do not intend to sound disparaging, in fact, [it displayed that] he was a true professional. To be heartless and ruthless for the furtherance of one's objective are inherent attributes required for the intelligence field. From the time that I was captured right up to date, I have repeatedly come across 'Coudert' types, i.e., covert operatives, from Indians to Pakistanis, Americans, Bangladeshis, and others.

Coudert made me narrate the events of my escape again and again, trying to poke holes in whatever I said. For my part I did not tell him everything, being aware of the fact that the less one speaks the less likely one is to be bombarded with follow-up queries. Although there was no apprehension on my part of getting trapped for whatever I told them was true. I simply left out the details that were irrelevant to my present situation. Throughout my sojourn at the US Consulate, I was aware that the Americans were really worried. They were obviously more worried about how the Indians would react to this than about me! But they also seemed to genuinely care for my wellbeing. I had clicked with them on a human level.

As I had requested, they brought me maps of India and Calcutta along with a Bradshaw railway guide and other paraphernalia, all of which I pored over in great detail. I did my homework well—I had to—my life was at stake. In this game there are no second chances: you either win or you die.

A car suspiciously pulled up outside the Consulate with some people sitting in it in civilian clothes. They seemed to be from the Indian intelligence and they probably were. I saw one of the men get off from the car and talk to a guard. The countdown had begun again; there was nothing that I could do but hope for the best. If they discovered that I was inside, the game was up. It was difficult for me to gauge from behind the curtains of the darkened room. I subsequently fell into a fitful sleep.

Morning brought both Coudert and Frank with it. They had gotten some clothes, toiletries, and shoes for me. Frank's clothes and shoes fitted me. One of Charles Coudert's shirts also fitted me. When I questioned them about the situation, Coudert replied that there was a 'conflict of interest' of sorts. He then told me that I would probably have to be shifted to another apartment in the evening, since the Indian employees would be back in office on Monday morning after the Sunday break. Of all the luck that had come my way, this was the most significant. It was sheer chance that I had walked into the American Consulate General on a Saturday, and hence had remained un-noticed by Indian eyes who would have certainly spotted me had it been a week day.

I also got to meet a few other Marines including Frank's boss who was a Staff Sergeant. From their conversation I became aware that a great debate about me was in motion. On one of the walls, the US Marine Code of Conduct was on display. One of them stated: 'if you become a prisoner, it is your duty to escape'. But Frank and the Staff Sergeant said something very telling: 'You do not worry, Sir, if these characters do not help you, we will. You are a soldier who has done his duty; we will do what we have to.'

I was very impressed by their conduct and bearing, any soldier would be proud of having met them. Camaraderie between soldiers is easily established; it is only when they come up against politicians and diplomats that soldiers run into blank walls. I have never forgotten their tremendous support—no politics were involved—only strong and clear statement of intent. Forty years later this still remains true. I celebrated my twenty-fifth birthday on 18 July 1971 with steak and pudding which the US Marines Detachment had very kindly brought. They also brought a small cake with a candle.

Except for the occasional visitor, I was left to myself the whole of Sunday, well stocked with books, newspapers and magazines. Packs of combat rations had been stocked up for me by the Marines and whenever I felt hungry, which was very often, I opened one of them. It seemed delicious after the POW Camp food.

As the evening approached, I was aware of a growing constriction in my stomach as I faced the possibility of another sojourn through the gauntlet that was camped at the doorsteps of the Consulate. I was constantly drawn to the window to peer outside to see whether there was any visible sign of increased vigilance by the Indian security elements but there did not seem to be any unusual activity going on. It was too good to be true. Charles Coudert came in the evening with another gentleman. He was tall and had a French beard. I think his name was Dan Thiel (pronounced Thal). We rehearsed what we were supposed to do as we got into the car that would take me to the apartment where I was to stay. With abated breath we walked out to the waiting car parked in the porch of the building. I was to sit in between the two men. We came out of the premises and turned right, both men constantly looking for any signs of curiosity by the police cordon outside. We turned left at the next corner and kept going. This was one trip where I was not really aware of my surroundings. The threat of discovery was ominous. We cruised into the grounds of an apartment building and then we were in the garage. We walked around to the front of the building and there was a policeman. We continued walking. The policeman gave us a cursory look, and then we were climbing up the stairs. On the second floor we were joined by a lady, someone I took to be one of the lady secretaries from the Consulate. Obviously the entire apartment block was occupied by American diplomats. A hurried confirmation from her that the apartment on the third floor was ready—and we were on our way.

There was a collective sigh of relief as we went in through the door of the apartment. I think it was only a few moments when we were joined by a Mr Paul Thibault.[2] He was in a follow-up car, obviously keeping our tail clear. He told us that he did not notice anything out of the ordinary—everything seemed to be normal.

The arrangement was that one of the Americans would stay with me at night, while during the day I was going to be on my own. After a while, Thibault and Coudert went away with promises of fetching me books and magazines the next day. Dan and I settled in for the night. Dan had been a navigator on an aircraft carrier before joining the Foreign Service. We chatted for a while. He talked about his wife and children. It was interesting to hear from him how much he missed his wife who was at that time teaching at the International School in Amman. Dan was very nice and considerate and was shocked to know that I did not drink—he had brought a whole case of beer with him. The POW Camp was gradually slipping away into memory; the thought of captivity was becoming a distant nightmare.

The first time I met Paul Thibault was when Charles Coudert introduced him to me on the evening of 18 July 1971 at the apartment. It was obviously a CIA 'safe house' set in an apartment block occupied by US diplomats working at the Consulate General. He was also definitely CIA, some rungs junior to Charles Coudert in rank, and certainly younger than him in age. I got the distinct impression that this was probably his first posting as a CIA operative. During our subsequent conversations over the nights that he spent with me at the apartment, there was enough to suggest that he had completed his training fairly recently. On the first night he was decidedly a little nervous in the beginning but then he opened up and we became good friends. We shared a common interest in books and music. He was extremely well-read, and even though I never got to know where he had graduated from, it was clear he came from an all-American family background and possessed a good college degree. The contrast between Paul Thibault and Charles Coudert was tremendous.

I was alone in the apartment for most of the day but after the first night in which Dan Theil was 'on duty', Paul came in the evenings to spend the night. Officially, he was there for my protection, but I had no illusions that he was also there to keep guard on me while the Americans decided what to do with me. By the second night we had become comfortable with each other, and he told me flatly that some people at the US Consulate General were opposed to helping me because of the diplomatic repercussions if the Indians found out. He also said that a majority of his colleagues, including Dan Theil, were up in arms in order to help me. They were never going to allow me to be handed over to the Indians, even if the Indians gave their assurance that I would not be maltreated. They all wanted to help me but they were bound by official dictates and diplomatic norms, and hence the delay in their decision. Paul Thibault was a very good man—he was ideal company for one who was living under the shadow of death.

Charles Coudert came to the apartment the following evening accompanied by Dan Theil. Although they had no news, they were expecting some very soon. Dan had brought some tuna fish sandwiches specially made for me along with some eggs and cheese. We enjoyed a feast and a nice chat. I had spent the day taking hot baths and scrubbing my feet with antiseptic. With the warm water flowing over my body, I could feel the tension flowing out. I was ready for another bout with nerves, if necessary. However I could sense that a decision one way or the other was coming to a head.

Next morning Paul came to take my photographs and to enquire what all I would require if I had to make it out on my own. I tried to list out all the things that I would need. I was scared but I was not going to expose my fears to them so I smiled while Paul took my picture.

Thibault commented how I could smile at a time like this. I told him about the saying written in the Ingall Hall of the Military Academy in Kakul: 'It is not what happens to you that matters but how you behave while it is happening'. I would be lying if I said I did not feel scared. I was scared but I could not afford to exhibit any signs of fear when I was on display as a soldier of a proud Army. That does not belie the fact that there were moments when I was extremely scared although I dared not show it.

On 21 July 1971, around 1 pm, Charles Coudert came and told me that I should brace myself with some bad news. But then in the next breath he said that there was also something which could be taken as good news. But first, he said, the bad news The American Government, after much deliberation, had decided that it could not take the risk of starting a diplomatic furore by helping me, howsoever much they sympathized with me. He said if I had walked into the US diplomatic premises in a third country, the situation would have been very different; I would be a fit case for 'political asylum'. He did not say so in outright terms, but what he implied was that had I been anywhere else besides India, they would have welcomed me wholeheartedly. He told me that from the enquiries that they had conducted about me in East Pakistan, it was not advisable for me to go back to Pakistan, but then, he said, that was my prerogative. He said that I should take this piece of news in good spirits since they had reached upon this decision after thrashing out the pros and cons and majority of the arguments had been in my favour. The good news, he said, was that an International Charity Organization had heard about me. They were sympathetic towards me and were willing to help me. A representative of the organization would come up to meet me. While leaving, he informed me that Charles Gordon, the US Consul General would shortly be coming up to the apartment to officially break the 'bad news' to me. Soon after, Charles Gordon came and I was formally informed of the US Government's decision. He wished me best of luck and left.

Again I was all alone. I felt panic rising in me. For a moment I thought that the Americans had sold me out to the Indians. I felt ashamed of feeling this way—the Americans after all had treated me so well. However, adhering to Coudert's council, I waited patiently.

There was a knock on the door. Then the key turned and the door opened. An American lady walked in holding a shopping bag. She did not bother to put up the charade of claiming that she had come from an International Charity Organization. She was one of the Secretaries at the US Consulate. In the bag were some clothes and a pair of sun glasses. She handed me an envelope which contained certain instructions and directions of known locations like bus terminals, railway stations etc., where the Indians were searching for me. It also contained 1000 Indian rupees. As per instructions, I burnt the letter after reading it. I scribbled a note of thanks for the Americans without signing my name. I looked apprehensively at the lady but she did not look nervous and gave me a smile of encouragement. We had to wait for some minutes before we could leave the apartment. I sat down and finished the food in the lunch pack that I had been eating before she came in. We discussed the ways and means to leave the apartment.

We got out of the apartment and went down the stairs. I was told to hold the shopping bag close to the right side of my face when we walked out on the porch to get to the car. The lady fumbled with the car keys for an instant but then she started the car and we drove out of the gate. We zigzagged through the city. I was to be dropped off at the Chowringee which is the main market. When we reached, with words of encouragement, she asked me to get off.

The heat and the humidity hit me outside. The fear of approaching doom began to rise in me all over again. I was alone in Calcutta, but this time not as destitute as I was the last time.

NOTES

1. Nearly 25 years later, in 1992, Charles Coudert come to Karachi and contacted me, requesting that I come over and meet him at the US Consulate General Chancery premises. We met and chatted over our Calcutta days. From the attention that he was getting at the US Consulate, it was obvious that he was fairly senior in the CIA hierarchy.

2. I met Paul Thibault again in 1990. He was serving as CIA's Station Head in Karachi. Many years later we met up again briefly. By this time Paul had left the CIA and had set up a real estate business somewhere near Boston.

11

RUN SILENT

It was now July. I was again alone in Calcutta. However, I was a transformed Ikram Sehgal from one who had walked into the US Consulate General earlier that month. I had entered barefoot, a destitute with hardly any clothes in my back and not a penny in my pocket. I walked out from there well clothed, well rested, wearing comfortable shoes and with some money to get around. The 1000 Indian Rupees seemed like a million at the time. All roads leading out of Calcutta were blocked. The buses and trains all over West Bengal and adjacent areas were being searched by determined men who had been given orders to go that extra mile to shoot and capture an adversary. The Americans had made it very clear—the Indians want you more dead than alive. However the Americans believed that the Indians still were of the opinion that I had headed west, or even south. They had been circulating my photograph at bus stops and railway stations, and every person exiting Calcutta was subjected to detailed scrutiny. Scores of people had been detained temporarily for further questioning, mostly Naxalities, because of my brief 'association' with Majumdar in the Agartala Jail. Because of the influx of hundreds of thousands of Bengali refugees, this did not excite much attention from the populace. That made it all the more difficult to break free from the city. What a change, once Calcutta had been a safe haven for me to reach—now it had become another prison to break out of.

You run silent, you run deep, and you do that in sequence, and even simultaneously.

But before you begin to run, you must plan your next spurt towards freedom.

You must not take a hasty step, you must think. Your life depends on it.

Freedom was still many heartbeats away, and the heart must not beat too fast, lest it gives you away. What was I to do now? Where was I to go from here? Having tasted the fruits of freedom, it would have been heartbreaking to be caught now.

The borders of East Pakistan were not too far away, less than twenty miles, but the exit and entry points were heavily guarded. One would certainly have to contend with several check posts. There was no way I could pass over unnoticed. The countryside was teeming with refugees and beyond the borders the entire area was sure to be infested with elements of the newly formed Mukti Bahini or 'Freedom Fighters'. I could only speak broken Bengali—in their hands I would get a short shrift as a 'Behari'. I had already had the experience once: my batman Mostafa got me through as an Urdu-speaking Bengali belonging to the Nawab of Dacca family. This time I was on my own. Because of the danger lurking on both sides of the eastern borders, I made up my mind not to risk an exit out of there into East Pakistan. Life would not have been worth the price of a bullet. Looking back on it now and the circumstances since I have come back to Pakistan, I think that was the sanest decision that I have ever made. Going east out of Calcutta or even trying to go north was a non-starter.

My maternal grandmother's family are Urdu-speaking Bengalis (as most Calcuttians used to be once upon a time) who came from Midnapore to the south of Calcutta. Husain Shaheed Suhrawardy and J.A. Rahim were my grandmother's first cousins. However the families had long shifted to Calcutta, and I knew nothing about the remaining family members except their names and other bits of stray information through conversations. The other option was more viable. My mother's elder sister was married in India to a Mr Sharif in Kishanganj to the northwest of Calcutta near the Nepalese border. Though I was sure the Indians were not aware of this fact, there was a distant possibility that they might have found out. Three of Sharif Uncle's children had been adopted by my maternal grandfather and were with him in Bogra in East Pakistan. I had visited Uncle Sharif way back in 1951 with my mother when I was only five years old. Although I did not know the exact location of the village, I had a distant memory of it. I was not sure whether my uncle's family would recognise me. Hence it was a gamble as to how I would be received by them and it was not worth taking it. Uncle Sharif was a big landowner and lived in his village home. They were located in the proximity of the international border with Nepal, and police would definitely be deployed there. Villagers are prone to be inquisitive at seeing a stranger. There was no possibility of my escaping their attention. I also knew that even if they were sympathetic towards me, they would have to give me up to the police for their own safety.

The immediate task before me was how to get out of Calcutta. Going anywhere by bus or train was ruled out. Who was going to give me a lift in their vehicle? In any case all vehicles exiting Calcutta were likely to undergo checking.

I turned into the busy market of Chowringee with a quick furtive glance over my shoulder to make sure that I was not being watched by somebody who could take away my freedom yet again. I wandered around, idly gazing at the shop's display windows, acting very much like a window-shopper, as my mind clicked over at great speed planning my next move. Examining all the possibilities and options I had gone over during my 'American' hiatus, suddenly my feverish mind became as clear as a crystal ball and I knew what I had to do. It meant taking a supreme gamble but then the stakes were very high. If the roads out of Calcutta were closed to me, then I must bypass them. Col. Nusrat's instructions kept echoing in my mind: 'think as they think; then out-think them.' The 'art of the unorthodox' in all its fineness! Would the Indians be watching the airport? Will they think it possible that I may in fact attempt to risk an aeroplane journey out of the city? The more I thought of it, the more I was convinced that this possibility had not occurred to them. They knew that I had no money . . . no clothes. They had not suspected my entry into the American Consulate General or they would have raised hell by now. By all accounts they obviously could not guess that I would have access to money, hence, they could not possibly imagine my plans.

I decided to take an Indian Airlines flight to New Delhi or any other place to the west of Calcutta. That would take me to an exit point out of India on the western Indo-Nepalese border and into Pakistan. When I look back on it, the major reason that made me decide to take the air-route out of Calcutta was because I was a pilot and instinctively aviation-minded. Moreover, there was no other way I could get out of Calcutta.

From the newspapers it was clear that the Pakistan High Commission in New Delhi was still functional. There was some cursory mention in a news item about tensions existing between the High Commissioner, Sajjad Haider, and his Deputy, Humayun Rasheed Chaudhry, a Bengali belonging to Sylhet in East Pakistan. It could be speculation or even Indian propaganda based on the defection of the Bengali staff of the Deputy High Commission in Calcutta. In fact Humayun Chaudhry's cousin, Kohinoor Chaudhry was married to my mother's cousin, Lt. Col. Qazi Golam Dastgir who subsequently became a Major General in the Bangladesh Army. Hence I had to stay clear of Humayun Chaudhry but the fact that there was a Defence Attaché (DA) at the High Commission was quite a beacon. At first I thought it was Brig. Ghulam Hussain who I did not know. But when it was confirmed to me that it was Brig. Ghulam Hussain Khan who I knew from the army, it clinched my decision. I had to get to him somehow. Delhi now became a clear-cut destination for me for all the right reasons.

Why did I choose Delhi and not Bombay (now Mumbai), an obvious choice given the fact that it was a port and a metropolitan city. Moreover I had some connection to Bombay, however tenuous. My late grandfather, Haji Abdul Karim Sehgal, had part of the contract to build the Marine Drive. My granduncle, Shaikh Mohammad Abdullah, had served as Chief Engineer at the Bombay Baroda Central India Railways.

During the course of my conversations with Paul Thibault and Dan Thiel I became quite clued in about the state affairs prevailing in Calcutta. From our subsequent chit chat, I had gathered that much more was afoot in India, particularly Calcutta than met the eye.

I took a taxi to the office of the Indian Airlines and confidently walked in. I purchased a ticket for an evening flight to New Delhi under the name of Mahboob Murtaza of 8, Royt Road, Calcutta. It was approximately 4 pm—the flight was to depart from Calcutta's Dum Dum Airport at 7.30 pm. Hence I had to wait for a few hours. If I had to be an air passenger, I would have to carry some light luggage so I went back to the Chowringee market to purchase some. In my nervousness I ended up overspending. I had money stashed away in different places on me and had to be careful while extracting it. 'Sajnis', a small store had a field day since most of the items that I bought were from there. The black wallet that I purchased from them is still with me through in complete tatters now; the only remaining keepsake of that endless day. To round off my 'new look' (I was now wearing jeans and a shirt) I went into a bookshop and bought a novel, *Carpetbaggers*, by Harold Robbins. I also bought an LP of Nancy Sinatra and Lee Hazlewood: *Summer Wine*, to hold in my hand.

When a fugitive is on the run, time for him must seem to stand still as it did for me that day. There was a limit to how much time can be wasted and although I tried my best to while away the hours, it was no use. By now I was fed up of Calcutta and wanted to get out of the city as fast as possible. I also had to avoid public areas. I decided to take a taxi and go to the airport, which in hindsight was a grave mistake. Even a small error on my part at this point could cost me my life.

Before I left for the airport I did something deliberately. I bought a Postcard depicting a Calcutta scene and wrote a short note to Major R.S. Uppal, Company Commander 430, Field Company 203, Army Engineer Regiment, Panagarh. I don't remember the exact words but they were something to the affect:

> You said you would break me and send me from the camp on my knees. You were right. I left the camp on my knees but on my own terms.

There was no bravado in those words—only cold pragmatism. This was deliberately done to keep the Indian attention focussed for my capture in the Calcutta area rather than elsewhere. If it also made Uppal's life a little more difficult it would be worth it.

Looking back, I was lucky that I was not picked up by the authorities at the airport. It was easy for me to remain unnoticed in the city had I stayed on. I could have even gone to a movie perhaps, reaching the airport just in time for the flight. I discovered that 'Escape, Evasion and Survival' curriculum had great holes in actual practice: certain tactics have to be learnt 'on-the-job'.

Once I got to the airport, I found there was a considerable delay in the departure of the flight, and that really compounded my troubles. It was not easy to look unobtrusive. Although Dum Dum Airport was not busy in the evenings, I felt hemmed in and claustrophobic. I tried not to wander around the airport lest I became conspicuous but I could not help it. It was simply impossible for me to sit in one place. All airports have security personnel, but at the Dum Dum Airport they seemed to lurk in every corner. As I got over my bout of nerves I could even identify some of them. I went to the restaurant and ordered some ice cream. My stomach was so tight and my throat so constricted that I could not swallow the ice cream, even the waiter noticed and commented on it. I was feeling nauseous.

In the restaurant a number of passengers waiting for the departing flight to Delhi were sitting. Among them was one Mr Pathak, a businessman. He struck up a conversation with me. He and the other passengers were loudly voicing their frustration at the delay. It seemed that this was normal for Indian Airlines in those days. For me his presence was lucky since I did not appear alone any more. By now I was a nervous wreck—but our small talk managed to somewhat calm me down and made me alert—I could make no slips at this moment. Pathak, who owned some chemical industry or the other in Ahmedabad was quite a talkative soul and seemed to revel in his lot. Because of his garrulous nature, he did not ask many questions. However, he did ask me what I did. I told him that I was working with my father who had a business in Lucknow. The only comment that he made was that from my physique I looked like an army officer. I was dumbstruck at this point and pleading a severe headache I begged to be excused from further conversation.

The flight was nearly two hours late. Eventually I boarded with the other grumbling passengers. The plane was not too full and luckily I got a window seat; the one next to me was empty. Pathak was sitting across the aisle. I looked out of the aircraft as it rolled down the runway, and my nervousness finally started to slip away. I lay back and slept for a while till an airhostess woke me up for some snacks. Once we were in the air I felt much more relaxed. I was hungry and feeling relaxed ate up everything on the plate. I had managed to get a travel brochure on Delhi at the airport in Calcutta and went over it in some detail. My immediate concern was where I would stay for the night in New Delhi.

While I was not an 'accidental tourist', I was certainly an inadvertent one. Delhi always conjures up images from history books. The political and financial centre of several empires of ancient and medieval India, most notably the Mughal Empire (AD 1526–1761), the city has an unusual charm that makes it unique among the capitals of the world. The Government of British India felt that it would be easier to administer the subcontinent from Delhi in northern India rather than from Calcutta, located on the eastern coast of India. While Mughal Emperor Shah Jahan had administered the construction and layout of Old Delhi, New Delhi was designed by Edwin Lutyens and Herbert Baker, leading British architects of that era. Constructed in the beginning of the twentieth century, it lies south of Old Delhi.

The Pakistan High Commission is located north of Nehru Gardens at Chanakyapuri. It was one of the first foreign missions to be built. The building is an impressive reflection of Mughal-Islamic architecture and at that time was one of the finest buildings in New Delhi. The Indira Gandhi International Airport is 15 kilometres north-west of Chanakyapuri.

Located in the midst of the diplomatic area, and given the sensitive prevailing situation, the Pakistan High Commission was bound to be surrounded by security personnel. Obviously it would have aroused their interest if I was found loitering in the vicinity without any seeming purpose. It was all very well for me to know where the High Commission was located but how was I to get there without arousing undue suspicion? To maintain clear and logical thinking in times of danger may be drilled into us, but when one is faced with a situation of this nature, it becomes a feat in itself. By now it was midnight and to ask the taxi driver to take me there would arouse suspicion. It could even prove to be fatal. I made up my mind to undertake the task in two stages. First I decided not to loiter around on the streets of Delhi at night and find a place to stay where I could be reasonably inconspicuous. I asked Pathak of a good hotel, and he told me that he normally stayed at the Lodi Hotel which was reasonable and comfortable. It was centrally located on Lodi Road. That was where he was going to stay on this trip too.

From the tourist map I gathered that most embassies were located in the Chanakyapuri area, and that the Asoka Hotel, a landmark in those days, was not too far away either. Obviously Asoka Hotel was expensive and would be subjected to greater scrutiny. So why not go to the Lodi Hotel? Moreover, I could share a taxi with Pathak, which would not only be economical but would not arouse undue suspicion. Hence Pathak and I shared a cab to Lodi Hotel. When we reached he did not let me pay for my share of the fare. At check in, I gave my address as 8, Royt Road, Calcutta. If the Indians ever decided to check up, let Zeenat Hamid do all the explaining! Since it was midnight the hotel clerk did not seem too interested. In any case some other guests were also checking in.

Although I now had a comfortable bed to lie on, sleep was far away. I was worried that since I was in India's capital city, hotels might be routinely checked at the registry which would give me away and send me back to prison. Hence I decided not to stay for too long and checked out early in the morning, around 5.30 am. I took a taxi to Asoka Hotel. Being a five-star hotel it was bound to have a round-the-clock coffee shop. As I waited for my tea to be served, a couple of men and some ladies with heavy makeup came in. From their get-up I was able to figure out that they were film stars. Guessing my silent assessment, the waiter confirmed that they were in fact movie stars and had come back from a shoot. They were used to having coffee and some snacks before going to bed and would sleep till late afternoon.

My timing for entering the Pakistan High Commission had to be perfect. While we were driving out from the Lodi Hotel, I told the taxi driver to show me some sights. With the fare ticking along on the taxi meter he was only too happy to oblige. Passing a large open area (Nehru Garden), I was told that the Chancery opposite was the Pakistan High Commission. I could see a couple of tents with policemen and an official looking car that was probably from the Intelligence Bureau (IB). Feigning the least interest I worked out that I had to enter the compound from the side where the wall was low. The other stroke of luck was that Asoka Hotel was not too far from the diplomatic compound, and if I approached it from that side I would not be visible to the police picket in front. If I waited too long to get into the Chancery premises the place would begin to fill up and someone might become curious.

I went over to the side wall of the Pakistan High Commission at about 7.30 am. Some children were playing there and upon seeing me became curious. I paid no attention to them and kept walking to the front of the Chancery building till I encountered some guards. Without identifying myself, I confidently told them that I wanted to see the Defence Attaché Brigadier Ghulam Hussain Khan. They were obviously shocked and nonplussed. They told me that he was not present at that time. I told them that I would wait for him outside his office. My appearance and confident demeanour must have impressed them. They asked me no further questions and took me straight up to the first floor of the building. Two of them waited with me in the corridor until the DA's personal staff came in after about half-an-hour. His PA (a JCO Head Clerk) immediately took charge of me in a no-nonsense fashion. Mohammad Hussain Rajput, a confident, self-assured person [he became PA to DG ISI a few years after he returned from India, and stayed at that post till he retired in 1989], sent the peon off to make tea for me. Stashing the bag that I was carrying in the Dressing Room that was attached to the DA's office, he informed me that Brig. Ghulam Hussain would be in office in about an hour or so. He said that he was not going to telephone him because the phone lines must most certainly be tapped. Sensible man!

I told him briefly that I had escaped from an Indian POW Camp at Panagarh. He was calm, cool and collected—and while exhibiting genuine concern at what I had gone through, he tried to make me comfortable and relaxed. In effect he was trying to assuage exactly what I was going through at the moment. For me this man was a Godsend. In the meantime he effectively sealed off my presence in the office from unwanted onlookers. Luckily the DA's office in all the embassies and high commissions are in a secluded area. The Pakistan Chancery comprised of a staff of over a 100 personnel, along with their families. Almost 35 to 40 per cent of them were Bengalis. Muhammad Hussain certainly did not desire unwanted onlookers to see me. There was enough reason to doubt their loyalty, what else could one expect after the Dacca crackdown of 25 March? By this time the sudden burst of adrenaline after the sleepless night had got to me and I was feeling quite drowsy. He fussed over me and insisted that I stretch out on the sofa till the arrival of the Defence Attaché.

I had not realized until that moment how exhausted I was and dozed off into a fitful sleep!

12

DELHI DAYS

Pakistan's Defence Attaché (DA) in India Brig. Ghulam Hassan Khan,[1] walked into his office shortly after 9.30 am. For me, the first interaction with a Pakistan Army officer after escaping from the Indian POW Camp was very welcome; the second stage of my quest for freedom was complete. No longer would all of us be 'missing presumed dead'. Moreover Pakistan could now officially ask India about their safety and welfare. There was another military officer under cover at the High Commission, although, I was never introduced to him or for that matter informed about him.

I cannot recollect with certainty when I had met Brig. Ghulam Hassan Khan; it was probably when he was a Major and my father's student in the 'Tactical Wing' of Command and Staff College Quetta. My real acquaintance with Ghulam Hassan Khan began when he was Commanding Officer 16 Punjab[2] at Quetta. My roommate, good friend and platoon mate at the PMA Lt. Sher Afghan was one of Ghulam Hassan's officers when I landed up in Quetta to do the Officer Weapon and Junior Tactics Course in early 1967. Since the food at the Infantry School Student Officer's Mess was quite awful, I and my roommate Lt. Ahsan ul Haq who was also my platoon mate decided to request 'Sheri' if we could attach ourselves to the 16 Punjab Mess which was next door to our barracks. When his CO, the then Lt. Col. Ghulam Hassan Khan, asked on what grounds, my rather dubious claim was that 'Shahjehanpur Levy', the forerunner of '40th Pathans' [that eventually became 16 Punjab], had an affiliation with 2E Bengal, my parent unit before 1857. Col. Hassan had laughed at our obvious subterfuge and had granted us permission. We got excellent food and excellent service. Maj. Ghulam Hassan Khan, SJ, was promoted to Lt. Col. in October 1965 and given command of 16 Punjab. In December 1967 he was posted as General Staff Officer, Military Intelligence Directorate where he served for two years (1968–1969). Promoted to the rank of Colonel, he was posted as Defence Attaché (with the local rank of Brig.) to Delhi when I reached him on 22 July 1971.

All of us who were incarcerated in the Panagarh POW Camp had been given up for dead. Obviously the Indians had kept it absolutely secret: officially the POW Camp did not exist. How could they explain to the world that despite there being no hostilities between Pakistan and India, they were holding soldiers of the Pakistan Army as Prisoners of War? This was illegal in every sense of the word. The Indians had managed to keep it secret from the Pakistan Defence Attaché in spite of his network of contacts.

Brig. Ghulam Hassan Khan made me write everything down painstakingly and had it typed out before asking me even more searching questions based on what I had put down on paper. Because of my mixed parentage the DA had to display caution, and I do not blame him for doing so. It was not a comfortable fact to have a Punjabi father and Bengali mother, given the circumstances of those years—it is still uncomfortable after so many decades when both my parents are no more. There is a racial prejudice that defies description and it is not confined to Pakistan or India. It is especially directed against those of mixed parentage. For all purposes I was a renegade for having the audacity to stand up for the Bengalis. This prejudice is more Punjabi than Bengali, the Bengali prejudice is only a reaction.

Brig. Ghulam Hassan cross-questioned me until he was satisfied that what I was telling him was the truth. There was always this fear that I may be an Indian plant. In effect, I was being put under interrogation but in a sophisticated manner. I did not grudge him his caution. After the 'Ganga' incident, anything was possible. An Indian Airlines Fokker had been 'hijacked' in February 1971 by so-called Sikh rebels and then blown up on the tarmac at the Lahore airport. Unfortunately one of our main political leaders, Zulfikar Ali Bhutto who was travelling through the Lahore Airport was said to have given them encouragement. In the euphoria that the media created about the incident, Pakistan at that time failed to realize that this drama had been staged as part of a great game. Zulfikar Ali Bhutto's inadvertent presence there at the time had added to its impact. India used the hijacking as a pretext to ban all subsequent Pakistani flights to fly over its territory which lay in between East and West Pakistan, which was their intention. This was devastating particularly at that time. What the banning of over flights did was not only physically separate the two Wings of Pakistan but also caused psychological isolation from each other. Much later it was revealed that the entire drama was staged by RAW and Pakistan had fallen into the trap.

A few days after I reached the sanctuary in New Delhi the DA who had sent everything to Islamabad in coded message was summoned to Islamabad in person. I was instructed to stay put while he was gone. Quite literally, I was to be 'confined to the quarters' for my safety. Except for the two persons I was billeted to stay with, my only contact with Muhammad Hussain Rajput was through them. Boredom aside, they were days of great nervousness and anxiety. I was obviously anxious to know the future that awaited me. I was also keen to hear news about my parents and sister.

There were two small bedrooms in the small apartment with a living room that served as a drawing-cum-dining room with a small kitchenette. My two apartment mates were low-ranking but trusted employees of the Defence Attaché. They generously let me have one bedroom for myself and shared the other one. Unfortunately for me both were terrible cooks. The food alternated between *daal* (lentils) and vegetables. They could not bring food from outside the Chancery since that would attract attention. Rajput who was living with his family in one of the quarters on the Chancery premises could not send me anything regularly since that would also cause suspicion. However from time to time he did manage to get food for me from his home and I waited earnestly for such occasions.

August is a hot and sultry month and Delhi can become extremely uncomfortable. I had to keep the blinds shut—someone peeping in could not be risked. Venturing outside for some fresh air was out of the question. The waiting period sapped my patience. However my two apartment mates tried all they could to keep me occupied: bringing me newspapers and magazines, and sometimes at night they played cards with me. While they did not say so in so many words it was quite obvious that my compatriots were visibly getting agitated. From the newspapers that they brought for me, it was clear that the 'Jan Singh' planned to spend the early days of August in staging large demonstrations against Pakistan, surrounding the Pakistan High Commission as a focus of their attention.

I could sense a deep anxiety in my two mates and had the feeling that my security had somehow been compromised and my presence had become known to those of Bengali origin at the High Commission. Although they did not know my name, it would certainly leak out to the Indians that someone was staying under wraps in the Chancery premises. The Indians could very well put two-and-two together and know it was me. Much later, while reading the newspaper in Nepal in early August I came to know that the demonstrators had broken into the Chancery premises on 4 and 5 August and a group of them headed straight for the apartment that I had been staying in and had ransacked it. Obviously my presence had become known—whether they had identified me or not—I never came to know.

When the Defence Attaché came back, he did not summon me for a few days. I grew impatient and requested repeatedly to see him. When no reply was forthcoming for the second day running, I told my two apartment mates that I was going to go and meet him and did not care whether anybody saw me or not. My threat had the desired effect and that same night I was escorted to the DA's office. Brig. Ghulam Hassan seemed livid at seeing me and let it be known to me in choice words. He told me that I was an officer of the Pakistan Army and this sort of behaviour was not expected from me. The dressing down was delivered quietly but forcefully. It calmed the nervous energy that I was bursting with and I suddenly felt deflated. Frankly I really regretted my outburst; it was most unbecoming of me and I was duly chastened. Feeling sorry for myself I went back to my temporary abode and hunkered down again to wait. It was unfair on my part—I should have realized that Brig. Ghulam Hassan had been working on a number of options for my safe exit from India. All this became clear to me two days later when he meticulously went over the various options of exit with me. I was then told by him that I should prepare myself to move without due notice. He handed me 5000 Indian rupees as emergency fund.

Ghulam Hassan's Indian contacts had apprised him that a huge dragnet had been put out for someone but they thought it was a Naxalite chief and not a Pakistani. At first the search was confined mainly to the Calcutta area but was now being extended to the western borders. There was still no unusual activity to be seen in Delhi. On his visit to Pakistan, the DA had been in close consultation with Brig. Ghulam Gilani, the new DG of the ISI (Inter Services Intelligence). I was acquainted with Brig. Gilani from Dacca where he was serving as Chief of Staff to the Martial Law Administrator. I had flown him to his office on a number of occasions when the roads of Dacca were inaccessible because of protests. Another person brought into the loop of my escape plans was Brig. Iqbal Khan, Director Military Intelligence (DMI). He was promoted as GOC 33 Division and was serving there during the war with India. Of course I knew none of this till Gen. Iqbal Khan told me the details in 1972 when he became my GOC 33 Division (in the Thar Desert). Several other details were filled in years later by General Ghulam Hassan.

For my release, they had met General Yahya Khan who was serving as President and Commander-in-Chief of the Pakistan Army. General Iqbal told me that for security purposes, no one else was brought into the loop. Yahya was himself one of the escapees from a German POW Camp in Italy during the Second World War when he was a young lieutenant. Hence he took special interest in my safe return. The list of plans that the DA had worked out included obtaining a passport of a friendly country for me.

One very special favour to me was decreed by Gen. Yahya Khan. He tasked Brig. Ghulam Hassan that before he returned to Delhi, he should visit my parents in Karachi, assure them of my well being, and inform them that I shall be coming home soon. My parents had received no news of me for months. I was missing and presumed dead. But as all parents, they were not willing to accept my death until they had physically seen my body. From time to time they heard lurid stories about me, some of them spread by my own 'very good friends' who seemed to revel in hurting them.

My mother had been advised by someone that if every Thursday she visited the shrine of Abdullah Shah Ghazi that is situated in Clifton in Karachi, and prayed for my welfare, she would receive news of me on the eighth Thursday. My mother would walk barefoot from our house, which was about two or three miles from the shrine, to pray for me. Her Christian maid would accompany her. On the eighth Thursday when she returned home she found Brig. Ghulam Hassan sitting in the drawing room talking to my father. My mother later told me that she immediately knew from the look on my father's face that I was alive. Ghulam Hassan patiently answered all my mother's queries but cautioned them not to show any signs of the news that they had received. A small leak of information could put my life in jeopardy. He did not tell them that I was at the Pakistan High Commission. He especially urged them not to tell my sister who at that time was in Dacca with her husband. Brig. Ghulam Hassan told me later that he himself was overwhelmed with emotions when he was leaving my parents.

The DA's dressing room became on 'Operations Room' for me as I studied various options regarding my exit from India with the help of maps. This included my exiting from Bombay (now Mumbai) by air. Routes across the western border of India including the rail crossing at

Khokarpar or a camel ride across the desert near the Rahimyar Khan area were considered as options but were discarded very early on. The Wagah border crossing was straight away discarded because the Indians would be ready for this. However the various routes used by smugglers were considered. One serious plan was that I should masquerade as an Arab from one of the friendly countries. Turkish, Iranian and Jordanian options were discussed. More clothes were brought for me. I got the impression that Brig. Ghulam Hassan Khan was beginning to enjoy the process and coached me on several points. To keep the operation completely covert, only his PA was privy to the planning besides me.

We ultimately came to the conclusion that the safest way was to get to Nepal and obtain an emergency passport from the Pakistan Embassy there. This could not be issued at Delhi since that would provoke undue scrutiny at the Kathmandu Airport. I was to pose as a tea planter who had escaped from a Tea Estate in Sylhet. I was prepared to go alone but Ghulam Hassan felt that since the Indians were on the lookout for a lone person, it would be safer for me to be accompanied by someone else. He requisitioned the service of a young Indian, Ram Das, who was his agent and planned that he will travel with me along with his wife. She was to pose as my wife and he as my brother-in-law.

When I met Ram Das, I found him to be a young man in his early twenties. Frankly I did not trust this Indian agent and voiced my reservations to Ghulam Hassan. I was uncomfortable with the fact that Ram Das's wife was not trained in such matters and hence her reactions in times of emergency were unknown. However when I met Ram Das, he seemed calm, cool and collected. Brig. Ghulam Hassan seemed to have a lot of confidence in him and over the next few days I found out why. The man seemed to have ice in his veins. The DA calmed my misgivings and instructed me that I was to be under Ram Das's command throughout, until we reached Kathmandu. He made this very clear to me in Ram Das's presence.

I have often thought about this Indian couple who travelled with me from Delhi to Kathmandu but until now I have never put it down on paper. In fact I had spoken about it to only a few trusted friends. I did not even tell my children lest they boast about it to their friends as children are likely to do.

Our route was to be from New Delhi to Agra by road. In Agra we were to take a train from Raja ki Mandi Railway Station to Lucknow. At Lucknow we had to change trains to Gorakhpur. From Gorakhpur I was to go to the India-Nepal border at Nautanwa. From Nautanwa I was to cross the border into Nepal at Sananli and then take a bus to Kathmandu. The Pakistan Embassy in Kathmandu was my third sanctuary.

Brig. Ghulam Hassan then divulged something that he kept for the end. Two armed men were to join me at the Raja ki Mandi Railway Station in Agra and travel with me till my destination for purposes of my protection. He gave me the recognition code that I was to use at one of the waiting rooms of the station. I was instructed to eventually report to Dacca via Bangkok (or the air route decided for me in Kathmandu).

On 3 August 1971 we were ready to leave. The plan was to send out three cars ahead of us. Since the Indians had been waiting outside for purposes of surveillance, they were expected to follow the three cars. Brig. Ghulam Hassan would then take me and Ram Das himself in his car and drop us off at a public area. We went over our plan many times. Alternatives, in case we were separated were also discussed.

Before we finally took off that evening Ghulam Hassan sat me down to tell me something. For the first time he looked visibly uncomfortable. He told me that if I repeated what he was about to tell me, he would deny it. What he said shocked me although frankly I should have expected it. He said that in Dacca I would have to face a detailed enquiry regarding my 2E Bengal episode, and that while he was convinced about my loyalty, there were many who were sceptical. He told me that he feared for my safety once I returned to Pakistan. He said that if I went onto the US or any other country in the peculiar circumstances I found myself, he would not be surprised. And all this while I had been living under the illusion that I was a hero for escaping an Indian POW Camp! While I was certainly quite upset at the Army action in East Pakistan and could understand why the Bengali troops had revolted, not for a moment do I condone the killings of West Pakistani officers, in fact, I strongly condemn it. I believed then as I believe now, that the revolt was inevitable in the prevailing circumstances. That was their right of self-defence. My Catch-22 was that for me there was no other destination but Pakistan, and that meant West Pakistan. I told Brig. Ghulam Hassan flatly that I would get to Pakistan no matter what, and that even though I did not agree with what the Pakistan Army was doing in East Pakistan, I was still going to fight from the side of Pakistan if war broke out, which it was bound to eventually.

With tears in his eyes, Ghulam Hassan embraced me and assured me that he harboured no doubts regarding my integrity.

Clearly I had passed an 'Acid Test'!

NOTES

1. Brig. Ghulam Hassan Khan took over as Director MI Dte (1971–1973). He was given command of a Brigade in 1974 before being promoted to the rank of Maj. Gen. and given an Infantry Division (1974–1975). He was posted to the GHQ as Director General Military Training in 1975. Promoted to the rank of Lt. Gen. in 1977 Ghulam Hassan took over as Corps Commander at Mangla. After retirement from the army, General Ziaul Haq inducted Ghulam Hassan into his Cabinet. He was appointed Federal Minister for Production (1980–1981).
2. During the 1965 Indo-Pak War, 16 Punjab took the brunt of the Indian assault on Lahore at Dograi village on the Amritsar–Lahore road near Wagah. Fighting gallantly but against heavy odds, the Bn HQ and one company of 16 Punjab was cut off by Indian tanks, ostensibly belonging to 16 Delhi Cavalry. The CO 16 Punjab Lt. Col. Golwala was captured by the Indians.

13

RUN DEEP

There were many reasons for my not wanting to talk about my journey back home from Delhi. One of the two more important ones concerned the young Indian couple, Ram Das and Moni, who accompanied me from Delhi onwards.

After Brig. Ghulam Hassan dropped us off on the street, Ram Das and I took a taxi and then a bus to his apartment where I met his wife. They tried to make me feel as comfortable as possible, offering me their bed to sleep. I attempted to shut my eyes but sleep was far away, hence, I got up and we spent the night chatting till daybreak when it was time for us to leave. We took an in-city bus to the main bus terminal and got on to a bus going to Raja ki Mandi, one of the railway stations in Agra. The road was not smooth and it took us four hours to get there. I was reticent throughout our journey and there was a reason for it. Once we reached Raja ki Mandi Railway Station, I was to be escorted by two ex-army personnel up to my final destination which was Kathmandu. This was not known to my companions and was supposed to remain that way. Brig. Ghulam Hassan Khan never confided in me but I guessed that they were agents from the Special Service Group (Intelligence) or SSG (I). Not much is known about them; even less is talked about them. If the men were from SSG (I) then they belonged to a very special unit. Although their real names were not meant to be disclosed to me, I ultimately came to know them. The danger that we shared together had created a bond between us. I have no idea whether they lived and worked in Pakistan or in India, and frankly I never asked them. Whatever bits of information I gathered was through the snatches of conversation that we shared. I do not wish to expose them and put their interest in jeopardy. They were 'sleepers' in the real sense of the word but had been activated specifically for my protection.

For many years, the intelligence services in India, and probably others have been convinced that I belonged to either the ISI (Inter-Services Intelligence) or SSG (I). I do not know about the SSG (I) but the ISI was not too pleased when it was suggested in an interview on BBC in 2007 that I belonged to the ISI. Although I keep hearing it from time to time, both these premises are totally false. I came across what I believed to be SSG (I) for the first time in my life during my escape.

Raja ki Mandi is one of the many railway stations that are scattered all over Agra. This one is located in an old market area, probably from the times of the Mughals, known as Raja ki Mandi, literally 'Market of the King'. There are several railway stations in Agra, some of them are used for long-distance halt.

The names of my companions were Meher Khan and Nabi Baksh. Both were Punjabis and were posing as Mona Sikhs, i.e., they had no beard or long hair but wore the Kara or bracelet which is one of the religious requirements of the Sikhs. The Indian couple had no knowledge that these two would be escorting us all the way from Agra to Kathmandu. At least that was what I was told by Brig. Ghulam Hassan.

As instructed, I began to keep a lookout for them around midday near one of the waiting rooms. I was about to give up when Mehr Khan passed by me and gestured me to follow him—I did so at a safe distance. Nabi Baksh was waiting for me. The three of us walked casually towards a secluded corner. Once we had confirmed our identifications, we discussed our next move. By this time we had already bought our tickets to Kanpur which was to be our next stop. They told me that they were armed and also offered me a pistol but I declined. It would have been very difficult for me to hide it from the Indian couple. I had not realized just how well armed they were until we reached Kathmandu. They had on them an AK-47, three magazines, a pistol, and some grenades. It was planned that Mehr Khan and Nabi Baksh would position themselves at a safe distance from us preferably in other compartments. In case of emergency I would have to head for the front of the train where Nabi Baksh would be sitting. I could not stay away from the Indian couple for long hence our conversation was brief and to the point. We were not to meet again unless circumstances forced us to.

A railway platform is a great place to observe humanity. Certain personnel are common to all railway stations, such as porters (coolies), station master, his assistant, telegraph officer, linesman, along with the maintenance staff. Raja ki Mandi Railway Station in 1971 was no different. Brig. Ghulam Hassan had done his homework well. Because of the frequent traffic, no one paid attention to us. The hustle and bustle of the station kept us incognito, despite the fact that Agra had a large airbase and a military cantonment.

We had plans to undertake the train journey in stages: first to Kanpur, then Lucknow and onwards to Gorakhpur. From Gorakhpur we had to reach the Nepalese border at Nautanwa. The train that we had to catch was the fast express to Kanpur in the afternoon. This had been pre-arranged except that my companions did not know that we had company, and a deadly one at that. Since our journey was mostly during the daytime, I was to feign illness and 'sleep' on the overhead bunk. This was to ensure that no one engaged me in any kind of conversation. My 'brother-in-law' and 'wife' deliberately sat opposite me on the lower bunk. Nabi Baksh and Mehr Khan had disappeared like 'ghosts', though I did get a brief glimpse of Nabi Baksh getting into the compartment ahead of us. Since I had been awake all night, I actually dozed off.

When I woke up after a few hours, I saw signs of warning in the eyes of Ram Das and Moni looked terrified. I immediately knew that there was trouble. Despite the caution manifest in their expressions I could not help myself and peered down. What I saw shocked me. Below me, in full uniform, two JCOs of the Indian Army were sitting, bearing the shoulder patch of 'Eastern Command'. That was all we needed! There was no question of me to come down now. I was stuck until these two departed. There could always be this off-chance that they had heard about my escape. Too many soldiers had been visibly engaged in the dragnet for me in the first few days after my escape. Much later I came to know that the story being circulated was that I was being hunted down as an escaped Naxalite chief. Even though it was unlikely that they could put two-and-two together, why take a chance? My next few hours were spent very uncomfortably. I attempted to sleep again. Our story was that I was being taken to see a doctor in Lucknow and from there into the mountains for fresh air as per medical advice. In their casual chit-chat with my 'wife' and 'brother-in-law' they expressed their concern for my welfare. They even proffered advice as to where to go.

At such moments, time seems to stand still. All sorts of negative thoughts begin to flash through one's mind. While you sense a rising panic; you also quickly put your own further actions into perspective. There is no doubt as to what one has to do; yet any wrong move on my part could spell disaster. The major issue at such instances is to remain calm and not give in to panic. None of us could make any sort of move that would cause suspicion. While Ram Das managed to keep a calm exterior, one could feel the suppressed tension in Moni but that was understandable. However unlike from Panagarh to Delhi, where I was all alone, now I had trained people to protect me. Moreover, they were armed.

Calm down, Ikram Sehgal, I said to myself.

It seemed surreal that of all coincidences, two soldiers of the Eastern Command should come and sit next to us. Later Mehr Khan and Nabi Baksh said they had been extremely alarmed and had got down at an intermediate railway station to compare notes. They had decided to come closer to us just in case they were required. I wonder if these two JCOs ever came to know how close to death they had put themselves inadvertently. The JCOs finally got off at Kanpur.

By the time we reached Kanpur, I was fed up and decided to come down. I took a seat on the bunker opposite the couple. I began to observe Ram Das and Moni. While Ram Das was a cool customer, Moni impressed me greatly, despite her apparent panic. For the first time I began to look at her as an individual and not as just another expendable person that one comes across in our lives daily. The JCO episode bound the three of us—it is amazing how people tend to feel close to one another after sharing danger together. Before that Ram Das had been informal and casual but Moni and I had tended to be a little stiff and formal with each other. That episode made us a 'family' and we became comfortable with each other.

As per our plan we kept going till we arrived in Gorakhpur where we got off. We spent the rest of the evening at the railway station. Mehr Khan and Nabi Baksh were nowhere to be seen when we got onto the train late at night for Nautanwa.

It was a long halt and I strolled over to the market next to the railway station. Gorakhpur was an interesting place. A city of Uttar Pradesh, it is near the Nepalese border and is famous as a religious centre: the city was home to Buddhist, Hindu, Muslim, Jain and Sikh saints, in fact, it is named after the medieval saint Gorakhnat. Conquered by the Muslim ruler Muhammad Ghori in twelfth century AD, Gorakhpur region remained under the influence of Muslim rulers, such as Qutb-ud-din Aibak and Bahadur Shah Zafar for some centuries until it came under direct British control in 1803. It was one of the key cities where the Uprising of 1857 against the British took place. In the 20th century, Gorakhpur became a focal point during the Indian independence movement.

A branch of Indian Railways from Gorakhpur approaches the international border at Nautanwa, but passenger trains are infrequent on this line. We had got a ready connection to Nautanwa but once there we had to get across the Indo-Nepal border at Sanahi to the town of Bhairahawa. Siddharthanagar or Bhairahawa (as it was known in 1971) is the district's largest Indian city bordering Nepal. It is 265 km (165 miles) west of Nepal's capital Kathmandu.

We observed that although there were guards on both sides, mostly police personnel, no one walking across the border checkpoint was being stopped. We debated whether to walk across during daylight with confidence or wait for the night so that we could cross over in the cover of darkness. But that could also arouse suspicion. We finally decided to go ahead brazenly during day time and hoped for the best. It worked beautifully. Nobody gave us more than a cursory glance.

There was regular long-distance bus and truck service to Kathmandu. We would have taken this route but we took a chance and went to the airport. Daily flights of the Royal Nepal Airlines would take off for Kathmandu from the Gautam Buddha Airport which was located two kilometers from the city center. Luck seemed to be on our side: seats were available on the flight. We had money and I immediately took the decision to fly to Kathmandu since I wanted to get there as early as possible. While crossing the border I did not see Mehr Khan or Nabi Baksh, but I assumed that they would join up with us later.

I had run silent from Calcutta to Delhi.

From Delhi to Kathmandu I had to run deep.

14

KATHMANDU

I reached Kathmandu, the capital of Nepal with my 'wife' and 'brother-in-law'. The final instructions given to me by Brig. Ghulam Hassan were that we were to go by bus from Bhairhawa to Kathmandu; we took a chance and flew from Bhairhawa. As soon as we reached Kathmandu, I immediately contacted the Pakistan Embassy, thanks to the kind courtesy of some more 'friends'. My identity upon reaching Kathmandu changed. I was now 'Mansoor Ali', a manager at a tea estate in Sylhet, who, in evading the Mukti Bahini, had managed to escape across the border into India. This story was applicable since at that time lots of refugees had fled from East Pakistan into Nepal where they were residing in transit.

The ambassador was expecting my call and asked me to come and meet him the next morning. He said that he will ensure that someone was there to meet me at the gate. When we met, a hush-hush mechanism of contacting the Pakistan Embassy in the future was then set up for me. The situation seemed out of a spy story but without the 'high-tech'. The shackles of my bondage were now slowly but surely beginning to break away. The arrangement with my 'family' who had accompanied me from Delhi to Kathmandu was simple. Once I had made contact with the Pakistan Embassy in Kathmandu, I was to make a clean break from them and we were to go our own separate ways. We were not to make contact again—it was to be a clear 'divorce'. This is of course easier said than done. We had shared a part of our lives, living with the possibility of capture and even death hanging over us like a shadow, even if it was for a few days. In such circumstances one begins to live life by different rules and certainly not according to army rules. During the long period of tension and accompanying anxiousness, one begins to share snapshots of one's life, hopes and dreams.

With Ram Das and his wife, I stuck to my cover story. Unlike his wife who believed every word, Ram Das was somewhat sceptical as to its authenticity. He was aware of the fact that I could not tell them the truth and was understanding enough not to press me for details. What they told me about themselves was a fascinating tutorial of life in India as a minority. They were Muslims but had adopted Hindu names and belonged to the lower middle class. Since they had eloped while very young, they had to run far away from their hometown. Ram Das had a job of sorts but they knew they would be more vulnerable in a Muslim locality hence had taken a small one-room apartment in what was primarily a Hindu area and began to live there as Hindus. They seemed reasonably satisfied with their lives, and never expressed disappointment at their lot. Although three days is a short period to know about anybody but the experience that we shared made us very comfortable with each other. For their safety I have never spoken about them till now. Although we were instructed to part ways, we decided to meet up the next day.

I found myself a small hotel which would go with my identity and settled comfortably into my room. For the first time in months I saw no demons in my dreams. Kathmandu, the capital city of Nepal, is the urban core of the Kathmandu Valley situated in the Himalayas. In 1971, it had two sister cities, namely, Pattan (or Lalitpur) located 5 kilometres to its southeast, and Bhaktapur located 14 kilometres to its east. They are now part of greater Kathmandu. Kathmandu and its sister towns can trace their history to the period between 167 BC to the first century AD. It is now one large city, with an elevation of approximately 1400 metres (4600 ft.) in a bowl-shaped valley surrounded by four major mountains. Kathmandu is predominantly Hindu but also has a sizable Buddhist population.

Ataullah Jan, Pakistan's Ambassador to Nepal belonged to Gilgit. My meeting with him went off quite well. He was kind enough to provide me with plenty of money and instructions. I had been strictly instructed by Brig. Ghulam Hassan to stick to my cover story and not divulge the fact that I was an army officer. This was not because he was not trusted but to give him credibility in denying should the situation come to that. After all he was a diplomat and in the absence of a Defence Attaché or even an intelligence liaison he had to be the point-man. But he would have been very gullible if he had not guessed that I was an army officer. Once he asked me my profession; I told him blandly that I was a tea estate manager. I could see that he did not believe me but was polite enough to remain silent.

Ataullah deputed someone to help me move from my hotel to some other reasonable accommodation where I could be contacted easily. I was told to be very careful and restrict my visits to the embassy to the minimum, and that too only in case of emergency. He told me that the Indians had a fairly large intelligence set up in Kathmandu and had quite a run of the place. The Maoist revolution was still very much in the future. The situation has changed substantially in the last 40 years. Hence I had to be careful about my movement.

Emergency passport for me had to be made for which I needed photographs. The ambassador was aware of the fact that there were others who were assigned for my protection. I was told that under no circumstances were the two SSG boys to come near the embassy unless I was in trouble. He asked me to give a description of them and also set up a codeword identification for positive confirmation.

As freedom became visible on the horizon, the effects of prolonged tension began to play on my nerves. It was hard to believe that I was free. Due to security constraints I could not as yet communicate with my family, though I had managed to send some letters through a friend who was kind enough to post them for me from a third country for anonymity.

I purchased a large number of books and magazines and prepared myself to settle down in Kathmandu for a considerable while. Kathmandu in 1971 was simply overflowing with tourists, mostly 'hippies', who treated Nepal as a destination for pilgrimage of sorts. They probably headed for Nepal because of the availability of cheap opium.

My parting with the Indian couple was more emotional than I had anticipated which came as a surprise. It is amazing how even a few moments of sharing mutual danger together can create a bond between strangers. As per instructions, I had to break all contact with them from now henceforth. After I bade farewell to the couple, I made contact with the SSG (I) boys in a mosque as agreed. From them I collected the pistol and some ammunition. I decided not to take the AK-47 (they had collapsible butts) and the two grenades because those would be noticeable and, moreover, I could not leave them lying around in the hotel room.

It was in Nepal that I felt the first real pang of regret that my fellow POWs from Panagarh were not with me to enjoy the freedom that I was enjoying. I felt somewhat guilty and selfish that I should be sitting in comparative comfort while they were still undergoing the daily grind of prison routine. I shuddered at the thought of what they must have gone through on the day after my escape. I heard the graphic details later from Sadiq. I can only use the pages of this book to offer a sincere apology to them for the tortures and distress that they had to endure because of me. I hope that they are magnanimous in accepting them.

I had a lot of time on my hands and spent it in watching Indian movies, some of them a number of times over. Indian movies were very popular in Nepal. Since I was posing as a Pakistani businessman who was stranded in Nepal, it was but natural that I should while my time away by watching movies, reading books, magazines etc. I would go down to the hotel's dining hall for breakfast and indulge in desultory conversation with the young hotel manager. Invariably he would inform me of some place of tourist interest. The manager's name was Moni Singh and although he looked fairly young to me, I found out later that he had been married for two or three years and was a father of a child. Like most Nepalese children from affluent families, he had also gone to Calcutta in India for his schooling. Chinese food was very popular there.

A man who is impatient to get back to his country and has the spectre of captivity still haunting him cannot really enjoy himself even if he was in Paradise. Too many issues were nagging at me for me to relax and enjoy. Matters swiftly came to a head when it became apparent that the Indians were successful in their efforts to permanently block direct RNAC flights to Dacca which had previously been temporarily suspended. East Pakistan was systematically being cut off from the outside world. It was then that I experienced my first genuine scare. Two Indians, one of them a Sikh, with 'intelligence' written all over them paid a visit to the hotel and talked to the manager. They were engaged in conversation for a while after which I saw them go to a nearby hotel. It was obvious that they were checking up on something. Later, I engaged Moni in casual conversation and he told me that the two men had come on a periodic check for smugglers. I knew that this was simply an excuse. They may not have been checking specifically for me but certainly they were watching out for all Pakistanis.

Even though their visit may have been a routine one, I did not feel safe in Nepal anymore. I made a beeline for the embassy and told the honourable ambassador that I wanted to exit the country by any means. Ataullah Jan was visibly disturbed, but seemed unable to do anything. This was not what was needed. If the Indians found out about me, Nepal would become a trap from which it would be extremely difficult to extricate myself. The Nepalese-Tibetan border was very close and I had already done some research on its route. I seriously considered taking my chances with the Chinese rather than risk being caught in a corner from where the Indians could pluck me any time. The urgency in my voice must have got through to the ambassador because after giving it some thought he took the risk of contacting the local PIA manager, a Mr Naim Qureshi on telephone. Ataullah told him that a tea planter needed to take a flight out of Kathmandu at the earliest since a family member had suddenly fallen ill. The ambassador then gave me directions to contact Naim Qureshi who was to arrange my ticket for the first available flight to either Rangoon or Bangkok. I had earlier been instructed by the ambassador not to go near the PIA office as it was under surveillance.

Naim Qureshi turned out to be a gem of a man. Originally from the Frontier Force Regiment, [Maj.] Naim Qureshi took one look at me and declared that I had army written all over me. A soldier has a peculiar stance which is not easy to get rid of, hence, I was not very successful in posing as a tea planter. His declaration added to my anxiety. Naim Qureshi decided that I should immediately check out from the hotel and spend the rest of my days in Kathmandu at his house. He was taken aback when I told him that there were two others but without batting an eyelash he took it in his stride. He immediately vetoed my suggestion that they could continue to stay where they were staying. He wanted us to be together with him so that we could leave at short notice. He gave me directions from where he would pick the three of us up.

Naim Qureshi's family welcomed us with open arms. We stayed with them for two nights and a day and were smothered by them with affection. They gave us one of their bedrooms to stay, and Naim's wife prayed for our wellbeing and kept feeding us endlessly. We could not reveal our identities although it was clear that they knew who we were. I shall always remember them as the Qureshis of Nepal whose kindness, prayers and invaluable assistance helped in carrying me safely on the last lap of my journey home. Since I was departing in a hurry, the embassy was not able to arrange any foreign exchange for me. The ambassador had handed over all the arrangements to Naim Qureshi and the management of the PIA in Nepal. A letter was drafted for Aslam R. Khan, District Manager of PIA in Bangkok, instructing him to provide money and accommodation for us when we reached Bangkok. The letter was meant as confirmation to the message already sent out to him. The last night of my stay in Nepal was very comfortable although my nerves were fraught.

Since there was no direct flight till at least one day later, Naim Qureshi arranged for us to take a Union of Burma Airways (UBA) flight to Rangoon and from there onwards to Bangkok through a connecting flight. We were deliberately not to go near check-in or immigration; the PIA staff would arrange that. We bid our goodbyes with the Qureshis at the house and from there his staff took charge of us.

We boarded the UBA flight around 10.30 am without incident. It was a passenger cum cargo flight. We got into the aircraft from the cargo loading side with our boarding cards, thus, we managed to avoid immigration. In those days both immigration and security was lax, and we were carrying our AK-47 with a magazine, a pistol, and two grenades in our handbags. We had no choice and had to carry our weapons for protection. There was no backing out now. Either we got away or we were dead. In a way we had dared our luck and were successful. Forty years and many hijackings later, one cannot even dream of such foolhardiness.

How close we came to being caught was related to me by the Qureshis much later when I visited them in Lahore. Soon after we had left, his house was encircled by the Nepalese Police in jeeps. They never entered the house but kept a watch on it for some days. It seemed that they had received some sort of information regarding us but did not know our identities. This was indeed a close call but we had managed to beat the trap!

15

BANGKOK AND HOME

Armed to the teeth, the three of us reached Rangoon after the two hour UBA flight. While it was necessary to have the weapons at Kathmandu Airport, and even in the aircraft till we were airborne, we really did not need them now. But once onboard we could not dispose of them and were prepared for trouble ahead at the Rangoon Airport. We debated whether to carry them with us during our transit flight to Bangkok or abandon them in the aircraft when we disembarked. I decided against it because the weapons would then certainly be discovered when the aircraft was cleaned up by the cleaning staff. That would set off an immediate alarm—and possessing emergency passports, we would be the obvious suspects. Taking turns in the aircraft toilet we put all the weapons and ammunition into one bag. Unlike the present, security in those days was not a prime consideration; searching for weapons and hijackers at airports at that time was cursory. However there was always that chance that we might be body-searched along with our baggage which would certainly give us away. Our ammunition had become, from a necessary asset, to an unnecessary encumbrance for us. However we had to take the chance.

The three of us did not get off the aircraft together. Since the other two could not speak English, I decided to carry the bag with the ammunition. I was the only one to talk ourselves out of trouble. We needed to get fresh boarding passes for our onward journey to Bangkok. Fortunately this did not require us to go out of the transit lounge; we were handed our boarding passes along with twenty other passengers by the Thai airline staff. We counted the minutes till we boarded the flight to Bangkok. Contrary to our apprehensions, there was no security check in transit.

In Bangkok we were received by a very nice Thai ground hostess on behalf of the PIA Station Manager. She was holding a placard for a 'Mansoor Ali'. Things began to move fast when we were met by Saifullah Khan,[1] the Station Manager of PIA in the holding area before we had reached 'Immigration'. By some coincidence I knew him from Lahore where he was posted as Assistant Station Manager of PIA at the Lahore Airport in 1967–68. He had been serving as deputy to my uncle Ijaz Rasul Tajwar and I had met him and his beautiful wife many times socially. Upon seeing me Saifullah nearly collapsed with shock. Firstly, because he had heard that I was either dead or missing, and secondly, upon discovering that 'Mansoor Ali' was actually me. He had received instructions to arrange for our board and lodging until our flight out of Bangkok to Dacca.

We were met by Aslam R. Khan,[2] PIA's District Manager at the Asia Intercontinental where we were to be accommodated before travelling onwards to Dacca. When I saw Aslam Khan, I realized that I had also met him in Rawalpindi in 1968 where he was working as Manager for the Lufthansa Airlines. After settling us down at the hotel, Aslam Khan began with his queries. He asked me why I was masquerading as 'Mansoor Ali'. I was not too forthcoming in my replies. Aslam Khan then decided to inform the ad-hoc Defence Attaché (DA) in Thailand, Colonel Mujeebur Rahman,[3] Pakistan's Permanent Representative to the SEATO (South-East Area Treaty Organization).

Colonel Mujeebur Rahman soon visited us at the hotel. Since he wanted to talk to me privately, he asked me to have lunch with him at his house. There he asked me what I was doing in Bangkok and why were the three of us travelling under assumed names. I informed him that we were not supposed to divulge any information to anyone until we had reached Dacca. At this he immediately pulled his rank on me and ordered me to tell him the 'whole story'. I again politely declined, maintaining that I had been instructed to only respond to questions. I did not tell him that I had been instructed to only divulge information when I was provided with a code word from the enquirer. He was obviously not in the loop and was trying to muscle himself in. When he saw that he could not break me down, even by threats, we returned to the hotel where he took Mehr Khan and Nabi Baksh aside and gave them a verbal 'third degree'. They told him that while they respected his rank they had been told strictly to follow my instructions and could not reveal anything. In any case they had only been given instructions to protect me until I reached Dacca and nothing more. Furious at non-committal answers, Col. Mujeeb stormed off, threatening to have us court-martialled when we got to Pakistan.

He was back the next day and tried a new tack. All sugar and honey this time, he told us that he was proud of us since we had passed a 'crucial test'. Colonel Mujeebur Rahman insisted on taking me on a shopping spree on his own account, or should I say, the discretionary funds he had at his disposal as Defence Attaché. It was a Sunday and he took us to an open market from where I bought a good pair of boots (zippered in aviation style but higher on the ankles in the infantry mode). I also bought myself some clothes and Ray Ban glasses (knock-offs really). I was also given a whirlwind tour of Bangkok. Panagarh now seemed far removed even though the memories can never be erased. We then went to a club to have a meal with his family. By now my defences had somewhat broken down. I did open up a little to him and we discussed the state of affairs in East Pakistan and Dacca earlier in March that year. While the army had experienced some successes, attacks upon it both from within and outside the borders had been increasing. Colonel Mujeeb agreed that the propaganda was hostile and compromise would take some doing.

Though I spent a very short time in Bangkok, my conversations with Col. Mujeeb were far more extensive and covered a great deal of territory. While Col. Mujeeb was a very competent soldier, his views on how the Bengalis should be dealt with were both revealing and shocking. It was depressing to note that an outstanding professional harboured such extreme parochial views. He was viscerally opposed to the Bengalis. I find such sentiments even today. It is incongruous to consider someone you want as an equal partner, at least in theory if not practice, to fall in line and function as a second class citizen. When I asked him how he expected the majority of the population to accept the rule of the minority, he said that some things were ordained to be and that it was the fate of inferiors to be subservient to the superiors. It was clear that Col. Mujeeb was racially motivated. With such views prevailing even among the intelligentsia, how could one hope for the two Wings to remain united. It was clear that my Pakistan was dead; it was now a question of how the formalities of the division were tackled.

When he was certain that my guards were down, Col. Mujeeb finally asked me to tell him how I had got to India and what I was doing there. I caught on to his 'soft approach' of retrieving information out of me and politely told him that I was not in a position to do so. Thereupon he lost his temper and repeating in some detail what he intended for me once I was back in Pakistan, he stomped off. I never met him again. He subsequently became a three star general and was inducted in the Cabinet of General Ziaul Haq as Secretary, Information.

It was finally time to leave Bangkok and go home. Although at first I had thought of leaving the weapons with Col. Mujeeb but because of his attitude I decided to risk carrying them to Dacca. Hence once more we put the weapons in our hand luggage and carried them with us on to the aircraft. Flight Captain Anwar who was a friend of my father was to fly us to Dacca on PIA Boeing 707. We had already met since he was staying at the same hotel as us. I sat with him and Captain Baagza in the cockpit for the duration of our flight to Dacca. On the way we encountered a severe thunderstorm although the atmosphere was clear over Dacca. Through the clouds, I saw the lights of Dacca city. Home was now less than a heartbeat away. But was it really home or another transit stop until I reached West Pakistani soil?

The last lap of one's journey home is by far the hardest. For more reasons than one Bangkok had effectively served to calm my tensions quite a bit. But as the moments approached when I would finally step off the aircraft my anxieties came rushing back. Along with the joy of being back in relative safety, there was the fear of the unknown. As it turned out, my fears were justified.

Shortly before we landed in Dacca, I had a sustained moment of trepidation. I remembered vividly Brig. Ghulam Hassan's remarks to me: 'I would be subject to a lot of cynosure.' My views in any case were not in consonance with those prevailing in the Pakistan Army at that time. Hence it would not be correct for me to say that I was not anxious. . . . I was. However I was very clear in my mind about the situation in East Pakistan! I did not wish to go and witness what was happening to this part of my beautiful country—I was only going there because I had been ordered to do so. To me East Pakistan was home and yet I was well aware of the fact that as a Pakistani I was not welcome in my mother's country anymore. The time to take a final decision had drawn close. Such being my views, it made my situation even more difficult—I was certainly going to land myself into more trouble. Yet somehow I was determined to do the right thing. I had been through too much not to put my trust and faith in God completely. If I was right I would be vindicated; if I was wrong then I fully deserved any punishment meted out to me. But the question was: if I was to be adjudged 'guilty' as was being charged against me, with the accusation that I harboured 'soft' views regarding the Bengalis then my sympathy for them would certainly be construed as a rebellion; then why was I coming back to a place which I considered as 'home'? My dilemma was great: my father was a Punjabi and my mother a Bengali. Unfortunately

Punjabis and Bengalis were involved in annihilating each other and no end seemed to be in sight. What I had witnessed on 25 and 27 March in Dacca had shocked me. What I saw later with 4E Bengal and with 2E Bengal was no less shocking. I was in a no-win situation. There was no doubt that between 2 March 1971 and 25 March 1971, many excesses were perpetrated on innocent people belonging to West Pakistan and on those of non-Bengali origin.[4]

What does a man feel when he returns home after having undergone such a terrific experience? He is excited and expectant. As opposed to his reticence up till now, he wants to relate his experience of what he has undergone to every one. He thinks he has lived through a miracle, and indeed he has. The careful hand of God has seen him come safely home. He wants to embrace everyone with joy. He wants to lie down and kiss the soil that he thought he would never see again, be ever destined to walk over. Emotions well up in him. He thinks everyone is aware of the travails he has been through. But when he realizes that his enthusiasm is not being reciprocated, in fact, there is a sense of hostility and suspicion, he is not able to understand. It is then that he realizes that he has allowed his emotions to get the better of the cold professional in him. But then he calms himself down. He knows that he will soon have to face the cold, inhuman eyes of his interrogators who will try to cast holes in his narration.

Was East Pakistan 'home' in August 1971? Yes it was, but anybody who was living there in mid 1971 knew that it was only a matter of time before the country was torn asunder. I experienced this divisiveness first hand at the 2E Bengal. A unit which was totally Pakistani had rebelled. Its transformation from a loyal unit [in February] to becoming rebels in only two months was shocking. I was going home but to a home that was only temporary. I walked off the aircraft onto the wet tarmac of the Dacca airport. The clock had turned full circle. I was back from where I had started. The odyssey was over; the inquisition was about to begin.

As I walked into the hands of my 'reception committee', one last drama occurred. The control tower had informed the Captain and we were to get off the aircraft before the others. As I walked down the gangway and stepped onto the tarmac carrying my bag, I became aware that a ring of soldiers led by an officer were pointing their guns at me. Before I could react, Nabi Baksh who was behind me had stepped in front of me and had his AK-47 out—so had Mehr Khan. All this happened in split seconds. Before any exchange of shots could begin, I quietly asked the officer to order his men to put their guns away. We would accompany him wherever he required us to go but with our weapons in our hands. Good sense prevailed. The officer being a professional realized that these heroics were unnecessary.

We were taken to a car—and the three of us were piled into the back—while the officer sat in front with the driver. The others followed behind us in three vehicles. Driving into the city, I was struck by the number of bunkers and check posts that had come up. This was a city under siege—in the grip of a civil war—and it was depressing. We stopped in front of one of the government buildings surrounded by barbed wire. An officer who was waiting for us informed me that this was the Headquarters of the Inter-Services Screening Committee (ISSC) and that Brig. Qadir, its Chief, was awaiting my arrival. Still carrying our weapons and our bags we went up a flight of stairs to Brig. Qadir's office. He was waiting outside and we shook hands. He then said to me: 'So you are the "Superstar".' I turned around and embraced Nabi Baksh and Mehr Khan, and handed over the bag containing my AK-47, pistol and grenades to them. I told them that their mission was over. Someone who they recognized as being from their set-up was also waiting for them. As they embraced me, they had tears in their eyes. Mehr Khan said to me: '*Khuda Hafiz, Sahib, Allah har waqt aap jaise daler bandey kay saath rahai ga*' (Goodbye Sahib, God will always be with a brave person like you).

I knew then that my journey back from oblivion was really over.

I have never forgotten Mehr Khan's words to me. God indeed has always looked over me!

NOTES

1. After his return from Bangkok, Saifullah Khan did not do too well in PIA and eventually retired in bad shape. His wife Shaila worked for me at my security company, SMS, for ten years. She left in 1998 to be with her son and daughter who had immigrated to the United States.

2. Aslam R. Khan eventually became Managing Director, PIA Investments, and then Managing Director, PIA. One of his crowning achievements is the saving of PIA's Roosevelt Hotel in Manhattan, New York, from being sold for tuppence. Till today he remains a good friend.

3. Colonel Mujeebur Rahman was promoted after the 1971 war. He became the official spokesperson for the government during General Ziaul Haq's rule, promoted to the rank of Major General, and appointed Federal Secretary Information.

4. On the morning of 4 March 1971, I was personally tasked by Commander Eastern Command Lt. Gen. Sahibzada Yaqub Khan to fly to Chittagong to find out what had occurred near the Chittagong Railway Station. Feroz Shah Colony and T&T Colony [both inhabited by people of Behari origin] had been burned to the ground.

Through the smoky haze I could see dozens of corpses lying around. There were many instances of rape, murder and loot during this period which served to inflame the feelings of West Pakistani troops already deployed in East Pakistan, and also of those who were arriving every day by air and sea. These feelings were further inflamed by lurid rumours embellishing the facts. Unfortunately both the Pakistan Army and the Mukti Bahini were involved in such acts of violence.

EPILOGUE

I had spent 99 days in Indian custody, escaping on the 100th day, but I had to spend 84 days under interrogation at the HQ Inter Services Screening Committee (ISSC) in Dacca. On 10 November 1971, I was charge-sheeted for 'overstaying leave' (i.e., beyond my joining time) and severely reprimanded. Two days later I flew to West Pakistan via Colombo for a few days leave with my parents in Lahore before reporting to the Army Aviation Base Dhamial in the Rawalpindi district.

The animosity towards me in Dhamial was overwhelming and quite understandable, but I was not resentful. However the fact that food was refused to me from the Army Aviation Mess has stayed with me as a bitter memory.

There was no question regarding my serving any further in Army Aviation even though Brig. Jabbar, the Base Commander, was insistent that I stay on. Brig. Naseerullah Khan Babar and a few others also sent word that I must remain. Because of the impending war, I requested for a posting to an infantry unit, preferably the 19 Punjab, my father's original unit. I was lucky in getting 44 Punjab. This unit had a core of 19 Punjabi officers but when I heard the name of the Commanding Officer (CO), Lt. Col. Mohammad Taj, I had grave apprehensions. He had been in Dacca leading the original assault breaking out of Dacca Cantonment on 25 March 1971. He was well-known for his abhorrence of Bengalis and I was half-Bengali.

On 27 November 1971, at 7 pm I got off the train at the Rahimyar Khan Railway Station and was received by Second Lieutenant Hanif Butt, 'Seenghwala', as I immediately began to call him because of the large lump on his forehead. He had a wonderful smile that came through despite his huge moustache. The battalion was concentrated in Tarinda, I was asked to see the CO immediately in his office dug-out. Colonel Taj lived up to his reputation. I was a Bengali as far as he was concerned and he would shoot me personally if I made a wrong move. He was going to give me D Company—not 'Delta' but 'Deserter'—as he called it because it had 25 men 'Absent Without Leave' and I was just the right man to command it.

My Senior JCO, Subedar Mohammad Khan, well briefed by the Subedar Major, acted defiant and dismissive as JCOs (Junior Commissioned Officers) are apt to do in such circumstances. I told him that I did not need him and he should report to the CO. But Mohammad Khan hung around till late evening, and after I was done with interviewing all the soldiers in my company, he came to me and said that he had made a mistake and would never repeat it. He lived up to his word. In fact he refused to serve further giving up his chance of becoming SM after I was dismissed from service two years later without any reasons given to me for this action.

When war broke out between India and Pakistan on 3 December 1971, as part of 60 Brigade and 33 Division, we were supposed to strike deep into the Indian desert, aiming for Jaisalmer. As it turned out this was a pipedream. With the Indians threatening to take Chor and Umarkot, and thus enter into the 'green belt', we ended up being force-marched south by trucks and train till we reached Mirpurkhas. We moved forward by foot from Mirpurkhas under incessant air attacks to provide reinforcement to the 55 Brigade of 18 Division at Umarkot and Chor. When we arrived, we found the units of 55 Brigade in shambles. While on the move the 44 Punjab brought down two Indian fighter jets, (my company bagged one), by concentrated machine gun fire, just short of Umarkot on 12 December 1971.

We reached the gun positions of both 26 Field and 40 Field Regiments near Chor. One battery was being commanded by Major Hamid Niaz, also an Army Aviator. They were virtually firing over open sights without any infantry on the ridges in front of them. Contrary to all training, we had our 'Orders (O) Group' in the gun position of Hamid Niaz's Battery. Two companies were formed up around midnight facing Sanohi Ridge where the enemy was believed to be deployed. Major Hamid Niaz handed us mugs of tea, cheerfully declaring that we might as well drink it since we were certainly going to be 'Shaheed' shortly. On the morning of 13 December 1971, at about 5.30 am, while the guns were still booming, Col. Taj came up to Sanohi Ridge and gave me 'battlefield promotion' to the rank of Major, taking the crown off his shoulders and putting it on mine. He had taken permission from the GOC.

There is no better therapy in the world than being in close proximity to soldiers that you are privileged to command. I was fortunate to get to fight a war in December 1971 soon after I had gone through interrogation/debriefing and been sent back to West Pakistan. To be posted to an infantry unit of 44 Punjab (now 4 Sindh) acted like balm upon my tortured soul. We were pulled out from the Forward Defensive Localities (FDL's) near Umarkot and Chor because of the Sindhi language disturbances that occurred in July–October 1972. Thereafter during the Balochistan operations that started from February 1973, with the arbitrary changeover of Governor Ghous Bakhsh Bizenjo by Governor Akbar Bugti, I remained in Balochistan throughout the counter-insurgency operations until I left the army in January 1974. This last service as an army officer in the field in extreme circumstances was a matter of great satisfaction to me personally.

Battlefield promotion is always to be cherished but my soldier's pride was restored by my beloved 'Delta Company' that was renamed 'Sehgal Company' by Col. Taj, particularly in the circumstances I was enmeshed. The fact that the mechanized rifle company still carries that name is something that will always be cherished by me.

My granddaughters Amaani and Elena will keep this memory alive.

AFTERWORD

One is always wise after the event is over.

So much could have gone wrong. A plan seldom materializes according to the script worked out by the planner, though in the end the results may turn out to be just as successful. Far too many mistakes were made by me in the implementation of the plan. Only through experience did I learn how many pitfalls existed. My luck held throughout—someone up there was looking over me. A successful escape was by no means an ideal escape: it had the elements of audacity bordering on stupidity, and yet I was lucky enough to somehow wade through them.

At the time of my escape though war had not as yet broken out, conditions leading towards it had developed between Pakistan and India. Other POWs who escaped or attempted to escape afterwards were faced with an infinitely harder task. They were brave men and it is to their credit that many succeeded in their goal. Even though a virtual state of anarchy was prevailing in West Bengal at the time, with the Indian Army and police deployed all over for internal security purposes, I had a much fairer chance of getting away than the successor prisoners. I was a pioneer of sorts, with all the advantages that a pioneer enjoys, and all the drawbacks that he has to encounter. In all cases there is always the mystery of the unknown.

The feeling of deep gratitude that I feel for those of my comrades that were there in spirit with me in the escape shall always remain with me. Their memory provided me with moral sustenance and encouragement which was invaluable.

Emotions are integral to humankind. A person who professes to be devoid of emotions is only an apology of a human being. However what needs to be avoided are emotions that begin to conflict with the cold, rational evaluation of one's mind when one is faced with danger. Hence keeping emotions in check serves to sharpen the analytical and logical reasoning of the mind.

Lord Viscount Wavell, the second last Viceroy of India, while talking about instincts stated: 'Some people have the irrational tenth like the kingfisher flashing across the surface of a pond.' That particular type of instinct escapes me but the fact remains that I was led by my instincts for some time and was proved correct.

When in danger, nerves become a great problem and utmost confidence is required. Moreover, patience is another prerequisite, and I have to admit that I am weak in both. The loneliness of the fugitive can be overwhelming. Fear remains paramount. Even when the path to freedom has been made secure, the fear of the unknown refuses to go away. But if one gives in to fear, one is liable to make mistakes, which can not only jeopardize one's freedom but even life itself. The mind needs to be honed towards purpose, evasion and survival. All of one's faculties must be engaged in observing, assessing, planning and putting the plans to successful implementation. One must be physically alert from any danger and have the ability to make the right response. While remaining calm outwardly one has to be like a coiled spring. For an infantryman this will need no elucidation; it is a merely the acid test of a soldier.

Incentive to escape is everything. It is simply a matter of convincing oneself that one's motivations are worth striving for to attempt an escape because it can cost you your life. When I made my escape attempt, I knew that there would be no second chance: either I would escape or get killed. The promise of a bullet provided proper incentive (to my heels) on the road to Calcutta.

Reliving the escape[1] was even more difficult than the tribulations that I suffered during my escape. I spent some very bitter moments during the course of my interrogation. There were moments when I thought that I was better off behind the walls of the POW Camp. But it did not need much analysis to judge that the venom displayed towards me by my erstwhile interrogators was because of orders given to them by higher-ups.

Majumdar, the Naxalite chief had a straightforward attitude towards life. If somebody hurts you, hurt him right back but harder so that he can never hurt you again. An enemy is an enemy and can never change. I remember his words but mostly in the context of the enemies of my country, not personal ones. It takes some doing, but in the end one can swallow one's vengeance. However, in life exceptions need to be made.

In conclusion, I must draw a moral from my journey back to freedom from the reaches of oblivion. Never allow yourself to become a prisoner in the hands of your enemy. If you do, then never lose your dignity, self-respect and sense of humour.

Freedom from captivity is worth risking one's life for.

NOTE

1. Most of my escape story was written while I was undergoing interrogation at the HQ Inter Services Screening Committee (ISSC) in Dacca [Dhaka] in 1971. A friendly clerk typed it out for me on rice paper while some of it was written by me in longhand and typed after the war by my company clerk. This was done deliberately to protect some people. Any indiscretion on my part at the time could have cost the lives of a number of people if the information was passed onto Indian hands. Therefore I chose not to mention any names even to my interrogators at the HQ ISSC. My reticence was later seen in a negative light; some of my interrogators came to the conclusion that I was hiding something.

APPENDIX

Notes on the Geneva Conventions

The present Geneva Conventions denotes the terms of agreement laid out in 1949 after the Second World War, although, it was established in 1864 and revised in 1906, 1929 and 1949. The 1949 Geneva Conventions established the standards of international law for the humanitarian treatment of victims of war. It categorically declares that a Prisoner of War (POW) may tell only his name, rank and number to the enemy and should not be forced into divulging any other information. To provide details of age was inserted as an afterthought for the benefit of the Red Cross. To quote the webpage of the International Commission for the Red Cross (ICRC):

> The Geneva Conventions and their Additional Protocols are international treaties at the core of international humanitarian law, the body of international law that regulates the conduct of armed conflict and seeks to limit its effects. They specifically protect people who are not taking part in the hostilities (civilians, health workers and aid workers) and those who are no longer participating in the hostilities, such as wounded, sick and shipwrecked soldiers and prisoners of war. The Conventions and their protocol call for measures to be taken to prevent or put an end to all breaches. They contain stringent rules to deal with what are known as 'grave breaches'. Those responsible for grave breaches must be sought, tried or extradited, whatever nationality they may hold.

Ratification growth of the Geneva Conventions was steady, with 74 states ratifying the Conventions during the 1950s. The present number of states ratifying the Geneva Conventions is 194 and is now almost universally applicable. Both India and Pakistan became signatories after the 1948–49 war that was fought between them over Kashmir.

Common to the four Geneva Conventions, or Common Article 3 as it is known, deals with situations of non-international armed conflicts. They include traditional civil wars, internal armed conflicts that spill over into other states, or internal conflicts in which third states or a multinational force intervenes alongside the government. Article 3 establishes fundamental rules from which no derogation is permitted. It requires:

1. Humane treatment for all persons in enemy hands, without any adverse distinction. It specifically prohibits murder, mutilation, torture, cruel, humiliating and degrading treatment, the taking of hostages and unfair trial.
2. The wounded, sick and shipwrecked be collected and cared for.

3. Grants the ICRC the right to offer its services to the parties engaged in the conflict.
4. Calls on the parties to the conflict to bring all or parts of the Geneva Conventions into force through so-called special agreements.
5. Recognizes that the application of these rules does not affect the legal status of the parties to the conflict.

Since the internal 'armed conflict' in East Pakistan had spilled over by default across the borders into India, Pakistan's status would probably come under the above category. However, the Indians were actively engaged in providing both material and manpower resources to the insurgents in East Pakistan. Those who had rebelled were collaborating with India that was actually engaged in waging a clandestine war against Pakistan, contrary to the norms of International Relations.

INDEX